HONORING DARKNESS

EMBRACE SHADOW WORK TO NOURISH AND GROW YOUR POWER

WINNIE CHAN WANG
JI W. CHOI, M.A.

Soulfully Aligned
Publishing

Copyright © 2022 by Winnie Chan Wang & Ji W. Choi

All rights reserved. Apart from any fair dealing for the purposes of research or private study, or criticism or review, as permitted under the Copyright, Designs, and Patents Act 1988, this publication may only be reproduced, stored, or transmitted, in any form or by any means, with the prior permission in writing of the copyright owner, or in the case of the reprographic reproduction in accordance with the terms of licensees issued by the Copyright Licensing Agency. Enquires concerning reproduction outside those terms should be sent to the publisher.

*This book is dedicated to all our soul brothers and sisters out there seeking the truth. Together, we make the world a better place by **integrating** our shadow with our light. After reading this book, you will gain so much clarity about who you are and gain compassion for human suffering.*

I love my heart and soul.

I love all humanity.

Join hearts and souls together.

Love peace and harmony.

∼∼ Dr. & Master Zhi Gang Sha

"Compassion is not a relationship between the healer and the wounded. It's a relationship between equals. Only when we know our own darkness well can we be present with the darkness of others. Compassion becomes real when we recognize our shared humanity."

∼∼ Pema Chodron

CONTENTS

Foreword — ix
Preface — xi

PART I
Introduction

1. 1.1 What Is Shadow Work? — 3
2. 1.2 Why Do Shadow Work? — 5
3. 1.3 Turbulence Ahead! Before We Dive in: Brace, Brace! — 12
4. 1.4 The Oneness Of This Book — 15

PART II
Winnie's Journey Into Her Shadows

5. 2.1 Shadow Of Love: Rejection, Isolation, Loneliness and Grief — 19
6. 2.2 Shadow of Forgiveness: Anger, Holding Grudges, Hate, And Resentment — 31
7. 2.3 Shadow Of Compassion: Not listening, Understanding, And Accepting Of Self And Others — 40
8. 2.4 Shadow Of Light: Fear And Doubts — 51
9. 2.5 Shadow Of Humility: Ego, Arrogance, Unworthiness, Judgment, Competition, and Comparison — 63
10. 2.6 Shadow Of Harmony: Drama Seeking And Conflict Creating — 73

11. 2.7   85
Shadow Of Flourishing: Lack And Scarcity Mindset

12. 2.8   96
Shadow Of Gratitude: Taking Everything For Granted

13. 2.9   107
Shadow Of Service: Manipulating And Taking Advantage Of Others

14. 2.10   123
Shadow Of Enlightenment: Shame, Not Knowing And Avoiding Our Divinity, Resistant To The God/Source/Universe Plan

PART III
Ji's Journey Into Her Shadows

15. 3.1   139
Shadow Of Love: Rejection, Isolation, Loneliness and Grief

16. 3.2   146
Shadow Of Forgiveness: Anger, Holding Grudges, Hate, And Resentment

17. 3.3   156
Shadow Of Compassion: Not Listening, Understanding, And Accepting Of Self And Others

18. 3.4   162
Shadow Of Light: Fear And Doubts

19. 3.5   170
Shadow Of Humility: Ego, Arrogance, Unworthiness, Judgment, Competition, and Comparison

20. 3.6   184
Shadow Of Harmony: Drama Seeking And Conflict Creating

21. 3.7   191
Shadow Of Flourishing: Lack And Scarcity Mindset

22. 3.8   199
Shadow Of Gratitude: Taking Everything For Granted

23. 3.9   211
Shadow Of Service: Manipulating And Taking Advantage Of Others

24. 3.10   217
Shadow Of Enlightenment: Shame, Not Knowing And Avoiding Our Divinity, Resistant To The God/Source/Universe Plan

PART IV
The Treasures Of Shadow Work

25. 4.1   231
    Winnie's Gifts From Shadow Work

26. 4.2   248
    Ji's Gifts From Shadow Work

27. 4.3   256
    The Gift Of Awakening To The Greatest Love From Birthing This Book: 1+1=3

28. 4.4   265
    Turning My Darkness Into Safety And Kindness

29. 4.5   281
    Message From Spirit

30. 4.6   283
    Tribute To Carl Jung

About the Author   285
About the Author   287

FOREWORD

WRITTEN BY B. RAVEN LEE, PH.D.

The sole purpose of human existence is to kindle a light in the darkness of mere being.
C. G. Jung

Trust your wounds . . . they are where the light can enter.
Rumi

I am grateful for the trust bestowed upon me for over four decades as a transpersonal therapist and guide for those on a journey of awakening to their true self. Winnie is one of these courageous souls who answered her call to grow beyond her identity and beliefs.

We are shaped by our familial, societal, and cultural stories, which can keep us in a box to do the "right thing" to be accepted and successful in our world. However, there comes a time when our authentic selves can no longer be suppressed, and we are thrust into a crisis to break free from what has bound us.

I met Winnie at a time of crisis and inner searching. I was touched by her genuine desire to change and grow. Our journey together awakened her to this light that Jung wrote about, but also took her to the depths of shadow work, facing emotions that she had feared and judged negatively.

This book is the fruit of her labyrinthine journey of illuminating her fears, sadness, anger, and insecurities... and finding her voice and passion as a healer. Our shadows need the light to be witnessed, embraced, understood, and transformed. Winnie has created a template based on ancient Taoist wisdom of the ten attributes as a touchstone to anchor us as we navigate the darkness of our stories.

May this book be a guide for you to awaken to your light.

With joy,

B. Raven Lee, Ph.D.

PREFACE

BACKGROUND

Shadow work is the act of willingly facing the deepest darkest parts of our soul that we have learned to suppress. By looking at our shadows, we learn to become whole by integrating them with our light. In the science community, this can be traced back to the work of Swiss psychoanalyst Carl Jung. In the spiritual community, this has roots in Tantric meditations and practices. The shadow work in this book is a combination of self-reflection at the mind level and contemplation at the spiritual level.

This book presents a systematic approach to shadow work of the "Ten Greatest Shadows" built on top of Dr. and Master Zhi Gang Sha's teachings on the "Ten Da 大", or the ten greatest source attributes.

TEN GREATEST ATTRIBUTES AND *TEN GREATEST SHADOWS*

1. Love
Grief, rejection, isolation, and loneliness

2. Forgiveness
Anger, holding grudges, hate, and resentment

3. Compassion
Suppression, not listening, understanding, or accepting of self and others

4. Light
Fear and doubts

5. Humility
Unworthiness, ego, arrogance, judgment, competition, and comparison

6. Harmony
Conflict creating and drama seeking

7. Flourishing
Lack and scarcity mindset

8. Gratitude
Entitlement and taking others, ourselves, and everything for granted

9. Service
Manipulation and taking advantage of others

10. Enlightenment

Shame, not knowing our divinity or source

Winnie has been a student of Master Sha since 2018. She downloaded the idea of writing a book on the Ten Shadows in June 2021 while attending the SLS Retreat "World Cup of Transformation".

Part 1 is an introduction to shadow work and the benefits of shadow work.

Part 2, Winnie guides you through the shadow work with her stories. She shares from the voice of a nurturing mom and a spiritual guide that dives deep. This book contains the deepest darkest parts of our lives, so grab a box of tissues.

Part 3, Ji shares her journey of her shadow work and shares from the voice of a daring sister. Consider her a friend that is doing the work *right alongside you*. Before writing this book, Ji had not taken Master Sha's classes or done the deep dive in Winnie's systematic approach. She **courageously** accepted Winnie's invitation. Winnie asked Ji, "Do you want to jump?" And Ji, without fully knowing what she was diving into, replied emphatically with a resounding **Yes!** Ji is an inspirational example that this system of shadow work delivers, and we hope you say Yes too!

Part 4, Winnie and Ji share the gifts of their individual journeys, and also the magic of supporting each other's paths. You get to witness the beautiful dance of Winnie being Ji's teacher and guide, and Ji being the student. Additionally, you see the teacher becoming the student, and the student becoming the teacher, as Ji's stories are the medicine and healing balm to Winnie's wounds.

May this book help every reader embrace and appreciate the gifts of their shadows and vibrate authenticity in every cell of their being.

In this book, we loosely refer to a higher power that created the universe, beyond human comprehension, as God / Source / Tao / One / universe. What is the Tao? Tao is nature's way. Tao is the sun that rises in the east. Tao is the cyclical nature of day and night. Tao is the true nature of all things. Tao cannot be fully explained. Tao is the emptiness of the void and the infinity of all forms.

In Tao Te Ching, Chapter 1[1]:

"Mystery and manifestations

arise from the same source.

This source is called darkness.

Darkness within darkness.

The gateway to all understanding."

This book helps us step into the most authentic version of ourselves. We call this "becoming the fullest expression of the Tao." That means we know who we are, we trust who we are, we know our gifts, we know our purpose, and we love the totality of ourselves. Would you like to give up struggling and begin flourishing in what you came here to do?

---

1. Laozi, , and Stephen Mitchell. *Tao Te Ching: A New English Version*. New York, N.Y: Harper & Row, 1988. Print.
   *Every time we reference Tao Te Ching, it's the Stephen Mitchell translation.

PART I

INTRODUCTION

Ten Da

1. Love
2. Forgiveness
3. Compassion
4. Light
5. Humility
6. Harmony
7. Flourishing
8. Gratitude
9. Service
10. Enlightenment

Ten Shadows

1. Grief
2. Anger
3. Suppression
4. Fear
5. Unworthiness
6. Conflict
7. Scarcity
8. Entitlement
9. Manipulation
10. Shame

1.1

WHAT IS SHADOW WORK?

Before shadow work, we were both cold-hearted, grudge-holding, self-suppressing, fearful, arrogant and unworthy, competitive and judgmental, drama-causing, scarcity survival mindset, disconnected from our gifts, manipulative, shameful, and unconscious.

Ha!

1. For the hero's journey of how we overcome our heart walls, read chapter "Shadow of Love".

2. For how we overcome holding grudges, read chapter "Shadow of Forgiveness".

3. For how we stop suppressing our expression and start listening to ourselves, read chapter "Shadow of Compassion".

4. For how we shift our mindsets from fearful victim to co-creators, read chapter "Shadow of Light".

5. For how we overcome our arrogance and unworthiness, constantly judging, competing and comparing ourselves to others, read chapter "Shadow of Humility".

6. For how we break the cycle of conflict and drama, read chapter "Shadow of Harmony".

7. For how we overcome the scarcity and survival mindset, read chapter "Shadow of Flourishing".

8. For how we reconnect and appreciate our gifts, read chapter "Shadow of Gratitude".

9. For how we stop manipulating and taking advantage of others, read chapter "Shadow of Service".

10. For how we overcome our shame, read chapter "Shadow of Enlightenment".

1.2

WHY DO SHADOW WORK?

DEAREST READER,

*I*f Winnie had done the shadow work earlier, as outlined in this book, she would not have to endure the greatest trauma in her life—losing one of the most important people in her life, her best friend for 19 years, in a divorce—causing much damage to her physical body, losing hair, losing sleep, losing weight, and a spike in cholesterol and blood sugar.

If this book existed as a parenting must-read book, she might have healed her childhood trauma and been able to offer unconditional love to her two daughters instead of unconsciously passing her own trauma on to them. Let's face it, hurt people hurt people. Unhealed parents hurt their children unconsciously!

If Ji had done the shadow work earlier, she would not have grown numb to her own body, denied her inner knowing, nor repeated patterns of self-abandonment. She would've prevented years of self-sabotage and feeling completely lost, all by her own doing.

From the deepest part of our hearts and souls, we want to share our most painful mistakes (aka lessons) so that you can be inspired to graduate from your suffering too!

Shadow work is the greatest gift a human being can offer themselves, as well as their parents, their significant other, their children, their friends, and their community.

Imagine you are sitting at a campfire with us, and we are pouring our hearts and souls out to one another. We welcome you to this safe, non-judgmental space. How you find compassion in *our* struggles is how you find compassion for *your* struggles.

Because we are both nerds, we intend this to be both a book of stories and also one that provides a systematic approach to doing shadow work. Our goal is that you will allow us to be your mirror through story sharing. We hope this book will inspire you to do your shadow work, that reading about our juicy darkness will remove the stigma and give you the courage to face your shadow.

RESISTING SHADOW CREATES SUFFERING!

Hold on to these four equations that Winnie adapted from Shinzen Young's "Science of Enlightenment[1]":

1. Shadow x resistance = suffering

2. Shadow x equanimity = purification

3. Light x dwelling = frustration

4. Light x equanimity = fulfillment

When we **resist our shadow**, we create *suffering*. Equanimity is the radical acceptance of what is in the here and now. Understanding impermanence, when we let go of attachments or resistance, we allow our shadows to appear and disappear as we inhale and exhale. When we accept and release our shadow, it leads us to *purification*.

At the start of Ji's spiritual path, she was stuck in suffering. She resisted any shadows bubbling up, being afraid of what lies ahead if she dove into looking at her shadows. She would avoid and distract herself from every trigger, and deny anytime fear or envy would show up. With every cell in her body, she resisted surrendering to the process.

When we **dwell in the light** (because we are attached to looking good), we create *frustration*. When we accept and share our light, it leads us to *fulfillment*.

Let's briefly talk about "toxic positivity" and "spiritual escapism". At the beginning of Winnie's spiritual journey, she was so attached to the light that she would want to be around "good vibes only." She avoided people and situations that are lower vibrations, and she always wanted to escape the stress by retreating to solitude somewhere in nature or her bedroom. She wanted to be free of her marital conflicts and the stress of parenting. She wanted to meditate and dwell in peace and quiet or go to all these retreats to chant more mantras…

What she was actually doing was running away from her pain, from being a wife or a mom, and most importantly, from herself. She was practicing spirituality as a coping mechanism to avoid reality.

Now we understand that under patriarchy, we were programmed to prefer the light over the dark. Let us explain…

LAWS OF YIN YANG:

1. Yang and yin are opposites, like fire and water, sun and moon, masculine and feminine, light and shadow. Light is not better than shadow, like fire is not better than water, and masculine is not better than feminine. Under the patriarchy, we have suppressed the yin and preferred the yang. Society values success as how accomplished a person is rather than how grounded a person is.

2. Yang and yin are interdependent—yang needs yin, and yin needs yang—yin and yang cannot separate. In the body, the formless energy (qi) is yang, and the matter (blood) is yin. Yang is the commander of yin and yin is the anchor of yang. Yang moves yin, and yin nourishes yang. Yin needs yang to grow, and yang needs yin to grow.

3. Yang and yin are constantly transforming to each other. Day transforms to night, and night transforms to day. The new moon transforms to the full moon, and the full moon transforms to the new moon.

4. Within yang, there is yin. Within yin, there is yang. In the night, there are stars. In the day, there is shade.

We have more access to our divine light when we do shadow work. The more we are in touch with our divine light, the safer and deeper we can do shadow work. The people who cry the most also laugh the hardest. Deep shadow work also leads to the brightest light of healing.

When Winnie practiced love and light without shadow work, she was dwelling in the light and scared of the dark. She was judgmental towards her friends and family that did not practice meditation and did not believe in unconditional love, forgiveness, compassion, light, and more. Because she was so righteous and a perfectionist, she was always trying to "fix" them, and she pushed her loved ones away. Her marriage failed, and she couldn't connect with her children. She couldn't be in Oneness with her loved ones who weren't in therapy or were addicted to video games.

When Winnie went through her divorce, her ego hit rock bottom, and she was crushed. She would think, "How can I claim to be a healer when I don't have love, peace, and harmony in my relationships?" She felt like a total imposter and hypocrite of everything she would preach. Suddenly, she found no choice but to face her darkness and delve into the deepest shadow work.

The body keeps the score. After years of prolonged numbness, Ji's body shut down. Ji was forced to surrender, and in her deepest suffering she sought medical help from Winnie. This led her to take her next big step into shadow work and purification.

FROM VICTIM TO CO-CREATOR

Shadow work is the process of **identifying** and **taking ownership** of the negative information that is causing suffering in health, relationships and finances. Once you become accountable for being the co-creator of all your negative experiences, for your part in creating your own suffering, you get to transform the negative karma into positive karma. One of the easiest ways to transform negative karma to positive karma is chanting mantras. Winnie's beloved spiritual teacher, Dr. and Master Zhi Gang Sha, teaches this one-sentence secret, "what we chant is what we become." He also created Tao calligraphy, which is spectacular in transforming negative soul-heart-mind-energy-body blockages to positive[2].

OWNING ALL OF OUR GIFTS

Everything is a gift. There is a gift in grief, anger, blocking, fear, jealousy, conflicts, shame, etc. The messages are encoded in the shadow. The instructions. The guidance. There is a wealth of information in our shadow that most of us have been ignoring, hiding, and running away from.

Another major benefit of doing shadow work is that by owning your shadow, you get less triggered by others' judgment and actions. Eventually, you get to appreciate every trigger as an opportunity to know the truth about yourself and empower yourself. Like a vaccine, once you have met the virus and made the antibodies, next time someone's darkness enters your vibrational field, instead of allowing their fear, anger, or shame to spread and knock us off our center, we get to meet the darkness with compassion. "Been there, done that. Your darkness does not trigger me because I have already met that darkness in me. I own it, I can transform it, and I can even share my light with you."

We are so excited to share our traumas, the responses that got us deeper into entanglements, and then our victorious recovery to liberation. Please picture us jumping up and down and screaming, "The only way out is through!"

We invite you to read this book KNOWING that your healing is going to look *totally different* than ours. This book in no way shows you how to heal but rather *empowers you* to take charge of your own journey and be the author of your life. Also, this book is intended to encourage you to use your voice and share your story so that we can learn from one another.

With greatest love and gratitude,

Winnie and Ji

1. Listen to Shinzen Young's Audiobook called "The Science of Enlightenment: Teachings & Meditations for Awakening through Self-Investigation" or visit www.shinzen.org
2. For a scientific definition of Karma, please check out "Tao Science: The Science, Wisdom, and Practice of Creation and Grand Unification" by quantum physicist and string theorist Dr. Rulin Xiu and Dr. & Master Zhi Gang Sha. To experience the healing power of Tao Calligraphy, please check out www.DrSha.com.

1.3

TURBULENCE AHEAD! BEFORE WE DIVE IN: BRACE, BRACE!

One last thing before we dive in... shadow work isn't a piece of cake. We want to give you some tips to brace yourself as you go on this bumpy but delicious journey to stay balanced.

Tip #1: "Hormone Hacking" - One of Winnie's "quick and dirty" tricks to get herself back to the center quickly is hormone hacking. Let's face it. Some of us are parents, or we have jobs. How do we go from crying our eyeballs out to quickly being functional pronto? Winnie lovingly calls this technique "hormone hacking" because why not hack your own body to produce the feel-good hormones? (Hormone hacking can also help overcome addictions and support a healthy immune system).

There are four feel-good hormones:

1. Dopamine: "reward" hormone

2. Oxytocin: "love" hormone

3. Serotonin: "mood stabilizer" hormone

4. Endorphin: "pain killer" hormone

Dopamine is the reward chemical that is released when we accomplish a task, experience something for the first time, celebrate small wins, and practice self-care activities. When you go to a new restaurant, try a new recipe, drive a new route to work, listen to a new song, or get something done and then celebrate small wins, you are releasing dopamine. One of our favorite ways to get dopamine is to look around and ask, "What can I clean now? Dishes? Fluff the pillows in the living room? Tidy up my desk?" *As a healing researcher, Winnie is always sharing cutting-edge revelations, featuring new authors, new healers, and new content on her social media. Get your Dopamine hit from her posts!*

Oxytocin is the love hormone that is released when we hold hands, hug, have sex, or give a compliment. *So every time you click like or comment on Winnie's posts, both of us get a hit of oxytocin!*

Endorphins are a pain killer that is released with laughter, exercise, dark chocolate, comedy, and essential oils. *When Winnie makes dumb videos or releases self-deprecating jokes for you to laugh at, the humor can release endorphins!*

Serotonin is a mood stabilizer that is released with exercise, sun, nature, and meditation. *When you follow the movement and meditations in our posts, you release tons of serotonin!*

Digging into our traumas can be an emotional rollercoaster. Make sure to balance shadow work with exercise + play + explore new things + laugh + hug + connections.

For a free 90-minute workshop on hormone hacking, check out the 4/28/2021 episode "Transmuting Trauma Response into Kindness", where we go over the four trauma responses, how to let go of judgment and self-attack, embrace and validate ourselves with kindness, find balance with hormone hacking, and receive a blessing of 明心見性 "Ming Xin Jian Xing" to discover our true nature: https://fb.watch/7iCA4ZmCOD/

For a library of 90-minute healing episodes (over 60 topics): https://mindfulhealingheart.com/circles

1.4

THE ONENESS OF THIS BOOK

We hope you enjoy the Oneness of this book. Winnie has four science degrees and a problem-solving engineer brain; Ji is a creative artist and dreams in beautiful colors. Winnie tells the heartbreak as a divorced parent; Ji tells the heartbreak as a child of divorce. Winnie was disconnected from her anger until she was 40; Ji had anger as her primary emotion as a coping mechanism for survival. Winnie was a people pleaser; Ji was a rebel who pushed back. The beauty of this book is it contains a diversity of perspectives, personalities, and talents. May this book bring Oneness of science and spirituality and help the readers appreciate the yin and yang of light and dark, structure and freedom.

Shall we begin?

PART II

WINNIE'S JOURNEY INTO HER SHADOWS

2.1

SHADOW OF LOVE: REJECTION, ISOLATION, LONELINESS AND GRIEF

*I*f dating apps existed back in 2002 when I met John at age 22, I would have had an impeccable resume. Big eyes, winning smile, 5'5, size small, bootylicious, long legs, sexy, perfect pitch, a love singing, dancing, hiking, traveling, a near-perfect GPA with 2 degrees from MIT, a financial analyst at Goldman Sachs, and a father being one of the most respected gastrointestinal surgeons who made enough money to pay for her degrees. On the outside, I was beautiful, outgoing, well educated, successful, and financially stable.

But I had unhealed childhood wounds that you wouldn't see on a dating app. As Taylor Swift said in her hit "Blank Space": "Cause darling, I'm a nightmare dressed like a daydream."

Like many, I grew up in a materialistic and chauvinistic culture that cared about looking good and saving face. Men are dominant over women, and sons are preferred over daughters. In 2020, the male to female ratio was 1:1.7 for the 15-24-year-old age group in China[1].

It is not uncommon for a mother-in-law to put pressure on a married woman to produce a son. A wife's duty is not complete until she produces a son who can carry on the family's last name and lineage.

The ideal man made enough money to provide for his family. The ideal woman was good looking and dedicated her life to serving her man and family. Girls who were pale, thin, and frail would attract a man who wanted to protect her and marry her. Feet altered by foot-binding were known as lotus feet, and the helplessness of a woman was considered a mark of feminine beauty and an economic status symbol. In the 19th century, 40-50% of all Chinese women had bound feet, and it has only been 100 years since this inhumane debilitating practice stopped[2]. Culturally though, Asian females were bred to be submissive and obedient. There was an expectation that we would 服侍 serve, wait upon, and take orders from others who are higher in the hierarchy. (The character 侍 is for serving the emperor—you get punished if you questioned authority). Fealty in Confucian terms: 1) people to government, 2) child to parent, 3) younger sibling to older sibling, 4) woman to man, 5) younger person to older person.

Growing up as the younger female daughter, I was expected to suppress my voice and obey everyone else. It didn't help that I was told I was fat and needed to lose weight since the time I was four years old. One can only imagine how worthless I grew up feeling and how I was bred to be a victim of codependent relationships. I had put my parents and men on pedestals—moreover, I was expected to, or I would be punished. When they talked, I always had to shut up and listen. Parents of that generation and culture were always right. They didn't listen to their children but punished them into compliance.

Gabor Mate says, "People have two needs: attachment and authenticity. When authenticity threatens attachment, attachment trumps authenticity." By the end of second grade, I was suicidal. A school teacher had accused me of cheating on a test because I was talking to the boy sitting next to me. Without asking for or listening to my side of the story, my mom spanked me for something I didn't do. (I was someone who never got lower than 90% on any of my work, why would I be copying from a C student?) If I dared to challenge her and talk back, I would just get spanked more times and harder. As a survival mechanism and to minimize the spankings, I learned to swallow everything I didn't deserve and didn't like, deny my truth and just shut up and endure the pain. The less I spoke up, the sooner the torture would be over. I felt life was unfair, nobody understood me, I was not worthy, I never got what I wanted, I didn't matter, and why bother living when life is hopeless? But who can blame their parents when that was how they were raised? This trauma of feeling not worthy of love, connection, and appreciation was passed down from grandparents to parents, from parents to children...

HEART WALLS = FEEL LESS = SOUL LOSS

Shamans are bridges between the material world and the Spirit World. Shamanic healers work with helping spirits to remove blockages at the spiritual and energetic levels to restore a person back to harmony. Since becoming a shamanic healer, I know that each time a person experiences trauma, they have a choice of closing their heart to feel less pain, but it also incurs at the expense of soul loss. It's like Voldemort in Harry Potter... a part of my soul left me each time there was a trauma, and I didn't want to feel the unbearable pain. (This is why it is important to work with a soul healer who can help you perform soul retrieval, or help you crack your heart open, or melt the walls to regain wholeness).

At 13, I was suicidal again. Another soul loss occurred after my parents moved me to a new school. Before I made friends, I was bullied by boys who would leave me notes of sexual harassment and tell me that they wanted to drink my milk and have lots of orgasms.

At 15, I suffered another soul loss when my parents sent me to boarding school, away from home, parents, friends, and everything I knew. I closed my heart so much that I would not feel the pain of missing anyone.

In the first year of my boarding school, I was racially bullied by a group of girls and endured a series of sexual harassment and abuse. By the end of the first year, I had another soul loss at 16 when a boyfriend broke my heart. By eleventh grade, I officially became numb and cold-hearted. Overworking became my addiction and trauma response. I became tough, rough, and super independent. Living alone, having no support network, and no concept of self-love or therapy. I was fully jaded and cynical before I even moved to New York.

THE TRAUMA BELOW THE SURFACE

The trauma that I can remember and that is visible to me is only the tip of the iceberg! Most of us have trauma that we can't even remember between the ages of 0-7. Did you know that 95-98% of our lives are run by the subconscious mind, which is mostly formed between the ages of 0-7? Until we practice conscious relationships, most of us are running some auto-pilot script formed based on our experiences from 0-7... That's why they say our relationship with our mom and dad sets the stage for every relationship that follows!

During a shamanic therapy session with Jay Dubois, I discovered that in my early childhood, I wanted to play with my dad, but my dad never made time for me. From that trauma, I developed "daddy issues". I believed my dad loved my brother more because, in our culture, sons were preferred over daughters. This later caused me to put men on a pedestal, and every time a man talked over me, I would get triggered and see it as "mansplaining". I would get angry when I am interrupted in the middle of a sentence by a man, but not by a woman. Not feeling understood, loved, and appreciated by my dad or my brother was a core wound that affected my relationship with all men.

My heart was basically closed after traumas I can and cannot remember. By the time I met John, I was showing up as a needy, demanding, manipulative, blaming victim in our relationship. I didn't love myself, so how can I receive anyone's love into my heart?

DISCONNECTING AND DISEMPOWERING MYSELF

By the time I met John, I was so exhausted from living in survival mode that I disempowered myself by putting him on a pedestal. I was so burned out that I just wanted him to take care of me. I didn't want any responsibilities, and I didn't want to live with the negative consequences of making wrong decisions. I completely gave up my power and discernment. I gave him the power to make decisions for me. It was a toxic codependent relationship. For 12 years, we lived "happily ever after". He played his role of rescuer, and I played the victim.

Then, in early 2015, when he and I disagreed on a major life choice, he made a decision that benefited him and hurt me. Trust was broken. I blamed him for everything (instead of taking accountability that I was the one who disempowered myself).

Before John's mom moved from Texas to California in 2014, John and I had never fought. When his mom moved to a home that was a short distance from our house, his unhealed childhood trauma was triggered. He and his mother would fight every single time she was at our house. My kids and I often hid in our rooms while John and his mom yelled. His mother wouldn't listen to John, much like my mother didn't listen to me, nor did I listen to my kids. Whereas I was a submissive Asian girl who had learned to swallow and just "take it" and endure, John would yell back to his mom. When his mom would leave, he would have so much anger that he continued to yell at the kids and me.

Many times he yelled, and I cried—I was trained to "take it" and endure whatever the authority figure gave me. It was most hurtful when the yelling would happen in front of our kids because I didn't want my daughters to grow up thinking that was an acceptable way for a man to treat a woman. But the most hurtful of all was when John yelled at me in front of my parents. That in itself was another trauma: how can my parents listen to a man yell at me and not say something? I remember that one time, we were on our way to our children's piano recital. We were running late, and John was trying to get everyone into the car. I honestly couldn't remember what he yelled at me for, but I remembered saying, "You can't yell at me like that. You can't treat me like a dog." I cried the whole car ride over. I was mad at John for yelling at me, but I was angrier at my parents' "failure to protect" me. How can they watch someone hurt their daughter and not stand up for me? (I was in victim mode back then and expected others to rescue me).

VICTIM AS A LACK OF SELF-LOVE

While I received a lot of undeserved and unprovoked yelling in the house, I became close with a male friend who was a really good listener. I trusted him, I communicated my intent for friendship, but it resulted in a rape. "Nice girls don't get angry." I remember when I was being violated, exactly what was going through my mind: "I can't believe this is happening, but what's the use in stopping it now? Just allow it to happen, just keep breathing, just relax your body so there is less pain. Wait till it is over. You never have to tell anyone, and you can just pretend this never happened. If you don't tell and he doesn't tell, then nobody would ever know, and life would go back to normal."

Right after the rape, he told me, "Oh, I thought you wanted it. I wouldn't have done it if I didn't think you wanted it." I was so mad at him for the violation, but I also allowed him to gaslight me into believing that I was responsible for what happened. And there was an abortion too.

I couldn't forgive myself for my stupidity of being at his house. "What's wrong with me? How can I be so dumb?" I blamed the playfulness and innocence of my inner child for getting me into trouble. I didn't trust her, and I locked my inner child in a closet. My ability to experience joy and fun evaporated.

Because I was raised with no boundaries, I continued the affair because having someone who would listen to me was intoxicating. I was addicted to receiving the love and attention that I was not giving myself or getting from John.

Because guilt-tripping, fear, and shame were used to domesticate me as a child, it became harder and harder to love myself. I was ashamed of myself and attacked myself constantly by calling myself a liar and a cheater. By 2017 I was having a nervous breakdown. I was angry about what John did to me—I *had to* hold onto the yelling and the grudge in order to *justify* my affair. I was also parenting my children from a place of fear. I was constantly living in the past (resentment towards John) and in the future (anxieties about my kids). Because I was not living in the now, I had a near-death car accident. In the moment of the crash, I had my first awakening. I couldn't keep living in the past and future. I needed to change.

My best friend Jessica Brodkin told me that she was also in a car accident, and she did three things that transformed her: 1) meditate daily 2) get Reiki or other spiritual healing 3) read the Power of Now by Eckhart Tolle. I followed her recipe.

In 2017, I received Integrated Shakti Reiki from Dr. Raven Lee, a channel of the divine feminine. When I first learned Reiki, I put this universal energy to bless my soups, my trips, my exams, and my parking spots. It was so magical that I manifested a teacher who could help me integrate spiritual healing into my TCM practice. In 2018 I met Taoist teacher Master Sha. He gave me a crown chakra blessing and taught me the 大愛 Da Ai Calligraphy ("Greatest Love"), and I went cold turkey on my 3.5-year addiction to Mr. Intoxicating. I ghosted and finally broke free from my rapist.

EMBRACING GRIEF AS A GIFT OF REALIGNMENT

Learning to love myself is the greatest love of all. For the years that followed, I did everything I could to open my heart further. In Master Sha's teachings, the heart is the Message Center. Our ability to receive depends on the openness of our hearts.

But I hadn't yet dealt with my mansplaining issues. Every time John would tell me something, I felt like he was trying to control me. I felt like he never listened to me, he was always right, and I was always wrong. He never compromised on anything, and during COVID, we fought. He was scared about everything and not comfortable with eating outdoors. He stopped taking walks with me. He got mad at me and got the kids to get mad at me for taking my mask off for 90 seconds for an outdoor photo. He got mad at me for getting into a car with a girlfriend. He wanted to set rules about everything, and all my old wounds came back: I didn't matter, I never got what I wanted, it's always his way or the highway. And one day, he told me he didn't see a way forward and *didn't want to do the work to keep this marriage going.*

When the separation happened in March 2021, it felt like the end of the world. For 19 years, John had been my rock, my best friend, my family (my parents live in Hong Kong, so I have no roots in this country), and my lover. The grief of losing him was like death. To let go of him, someone I spent half my life with, felt like letting go of me. But there was a part of me that knew I *could not afford to close my heart* to John. Because how I close my heart to John is also how I close my heart to myself, and how I close my heart to God. I decided that no matter how hard the stages of grief, I would allow myself to feel everything and ride the waves of denial, anger, bargaining, and depression.

For the days, weeks, and months that followed, I wrote him letters apologizing for everything I did wrong. I wrote him letters about the lessons I had learned. I wrote him letters appreciating everything he did for me. But he blocked me completely. I felt completely rejected. I felt like the 19 years meant nothing. He couldn't find anything to thank me for. I felt like he never saw me or appreciated me. The victim in me felt abandoned, discarded, and helpless. Nothing I did was ever good enough for him.

Rejection is protection and redirection. Grief is the feeling of love with nowhere to go. So every time I experience grief, I get to redirect the love to someone else, such as myself, my kids, parents, friends, clients, and community. Indeed the divorce brought many gifts, one of which was I healed my relationships with my mom, dad, and brother. The loss of my rock was so traumatic, and I knew I needed to cry on every shoulder that would listen. It also strengthened my relationships with all my teachers and therapists, as I asked for and accepted help from my support network. I learned to trust that everything happens for me and that I don't know better than God. Grief / abandonment / betrayal / any heart pain is a **_gift_**, showing up as a guidance for a realignment of my heart and soul.

BEING ALONE IS NOT GOOD OR BAD

Why are we so afraid of being alone? Solitude increases productivity because we don't have as many side conversations and distractions. Solitude sparks creativity because we can listen to our original ideas. Solitude brings clarity because we get to know ourselves better. Solitude gives us the highest degree of freedom, as we don't have to please anyone but ourselves. We can set our own schedule and deeply honor the needs, desires, and rhythms of our body, mind, and soul. Solitude gives us time to explore and develop our gifts. Every relationship will go through times of connection and disconnection. Rather than being sad about the disconnection or the end of a relationship, we can look at life as periods of alternating connection with the external world and internal world.

Exercise: write a letter to ourselves about our greatest grief of love unreceived. Then apply Byron Katie's "flip it around" method to see the emptiness of the grief[3]. To give you a one-minute hacker explanation, "I am mad at you" can be "You are mad at me" or "I am mad at myself" or "You are mad at yourself." This method is genius because by switching the nouns, we begin to loosen our roles and attachments to the suffering. I really can't do justice to her work, so please read her book!

Suggested music: "It Must Have Been Love" by Roxette. "Someone Like You" by Adele.

Hello. This is the voice of my grief.

I grieve for having no roots.

I grieve for having parents that live 12 time zones away.

I grieve losing a partner that I had imagined growing old with.

I grieve for being silenced, violated, and raped.

I grieve for broken dreams and helplessness.

I grieve for feeling unloved and unsupported.

I grieve being blocked and rejected.

I grieve for being misunderstood and blamed.

I grieve for feeling alienated from my children.

I grieve for saying goodbye to my home.

I grieve for the hopelessness that nothing I do is ever good enough to keep the people I love in my life.

And the loneliness and isolation that I bring to myself because I don't want to let other people see me in my grief.

<breathe>

It is me. It is me that rejects myself. It is me that abandoned myself. It is me that didn't seek help, didn't call my parents every day, didn't build a support network by being an active giver in my community. It is me that had let my partner down. It is me that silenced myself. It is me that didn't stand up and protect myself. It is me that disconnected myself from the home of my heart. It is me that put up heart walls that blocked myself from accessing the love from my higher self. It is me that judged, shamed, and attacked myself. It is me that didn't let other people in. It is me that didn't receive the love that others are willing to give. It is me that put myself through surviving on my own.

I am so sorry for all the grief I created for myself. I am grateful for the clarity in the emptiness of my suffering. *By realizing my role in my suffering*, I can *delete the conversations* that lead to my suffering. I love you as my teacher and my student, my parent, and my child, my lover, and my best friend.

Love,

Me.

Now it's your turn! Post your letter on Instagram and tag @HonoringDarkness or post on the free Honoring Darkness Facebook group to share your story in community!

#HonoringDarkness #GreatestGrief #ShadowWork

For a 90 minute episode on how to process the shadow of love, check out the 11/10/2021 episode on Self-abandonment. Kriya = reserve energy set. (fb.watch/an3lAOzWg9/)

---

1. "List of Countries by Sex Ratio." Wikipedia, en.wikipedia.org/wiki/List_of_countries_by_sex_ratio. Accessed 7 Mar. 2022.
2. "Foot Binding." Wikipedia, en.wikipedia.org/wiki/Foot_binding. Accessed 7 Mar. 2022
3. If you are not familiar with Byron Katie's method, please check out "A Mind at Home with Itself: How Asking Four Questions Can Free Your Mind, Open Your Heart, and Turn Your World Around"

2.2

SHADOW OF FORGIVENESS: ANGER, HOLDING GRUDGES, HATE, AND RESENTMENT

When I came to the United States for boarding school at 15, I left everything and everyone I knew behind—my country, my home, my family, and my friends. I felt like I had nobody to love me and support me, and I was the only person whom I could rely on.

When I was raped in early 2015, I felt like there was no one I could turn to. The man who got me pregnant became the only person I could trust, open my heart to, my best friend whom I felt safe to talk to. My husband, that was supposed to be my happily ever after, turned out to be a yeller. Just the sound of him opening and closing drawers, or the sound of him walking up the stairs, would generate a PTSD response in my body. Panic, shaking, shortness of breath, palpitations. I didn't feel safe at home, so the only thing I could do was escape. I activated my coping mechanism: work. I enrolled myself in my 4th degree—Masters in Oriental Medicine—so that I would be at school and studying at Starbucks.

Up until this point, I was the most loving stay-at-home mom. My daughters were my best friends. We cooked together, we hugged and kissed and laughed together. I was even the only parent that participated in kids' Taekwondo classes instead of playing on my iPhone! I was active at PTA, and I was always volunteering at every oppurtunity to be in my kids' classrooms and lives. When I went back to school full time, my kids felt abandoned, like they were losing their best friend.

When I decided to "come clean" and tell John about the affairs, he was so mad that he told the girls that "we are getting a divorce, and your mother did something and I don't know if I can ever trust her again." My children blamed me for the divorce, got really angry at me, and alienated me.

When you love someone, you also want to protect them. I love my girls, and I don't want to talk about age-inappropriate topics such as rape to help them understand the whole picture. I love John, and I never want to ruin his image by telling my girls about what their father did to me. I love my rapist, and I am never going to reveal his identity. Although he hurt me, he also supported me when I had no one to turn to, and he calmed me down through countless panic attacks.

(Quick side note: if you want your loved ones to turn to you when they are in trouble, don't yell at them. If you give someone fear or shame, you push them away from you, from *themselves*, into undesirable situations. I couldn't turn to John or my parents....)

SHALL WE TALK ABOUT FORGIVENESS?

Forgiving my rapist was the easiest—if my parents hadn't made me feel fat and undesirable since I was four, if John hadn't broken my trust and if he weren't a yeller, if I had chosen to heal my childhood wounds or gone to marriage counseling—this would not have happened.

Forgiving my parents was also easy. Parents and children have an unbreakable bond. It is easy to see how much my parents loved me, but their own unhealed traumas from their parents and their spouses were passed on to me. They did the best they could. They thought that sending their daughter away would give me the best future and did not know about the isolation it would cause me.

Forgiving John was hard. Forgiving John was hard because I had put him on a pedestal. When I met him at 22, he was my knight in shining armor—my provider, my protector, my rock, my everything. I really thought he was going to be the one growing old with me, changing my diaper, holding hands at the doctor's office, enjoying a quiet sunset. I wanted him to love me "no matter what", but he wasn't capable of loving me "no matter what".

He told me that relationships are transactional. If we were compatible, we could be together. If I don't have what he wants, then it's time to say goodbye.

It was triply painful because 1) he was the first to break the trust in the relationship, 2) he was the one who chose to end the marriage, 3) he blamed everything on me, so the kids are mad at me for breaking the family.

I can draw a timeline. I can collect evidence as to why I have every right in the world to be angry. But that only perpetuates my suffering.

> "When another person makes you suffer, it is because he suffers deeply within himself, and his suffering is spilling over. He does not need punishment; he needs help." — Thich Nhat Hanh.

Instead of seeing him as the perpetrator, I choose to see him as a victim. Everything he did was a trauma response. He has already done his best.

EASY TO SAY, SO HARD TO DO

The first months of co-parenting were so triggering. There was so much pain and anger that showed up every time I didn't get what I wanted! I didn't want a divorce. I didn't want to eat breakfast by myself on Mother's Day. I didn't want to come to pick up my kids at his house, only to discover another lady sitting in my seat in the car, sitting in my seat at the restaurant table, sitting in my seat on the living room couch, with John and *my kids*. It was only two months since we separated, and John took the four of them to a romantic English afternoon tea and hot tub.

It felt like a slap in the face as I was replaced as a mother. At this point, not only had he blamed the whole divorce on me, but he also blocked all communication from me except drop off and pick up. He even poured salt on my wounds, encouraging our daughters to bond with another woman while the kids were doing what their dads were doing: they didn't want to see me or hear from me. Not only was he not repairing the parental alienation he had caused, but his actions kept the kids from bonding with their mom. He would play video games with them on my nights, so even though the kids were in my house, they were still ignoring me and playing with their dad. Knowing that the plan was for me to take the kids out to breakfast before dropping them off on MLK day, he would tell the kids he had planned to cook a big breakfast (with another lady) so that my kids would turn me down for breakfast and I would have to eat alone.

Parental alienation isn't just bad-mouthing the other parent or making your kids choose which parent to have breakfast with. That is just the tip of the iceberg that is visible! Whatever anger, resentment, or attempts to block communication with the targeted parent is a poison in the pathogenic parent's vibrational field that children are inhaling while they are with them. Children are made to feel they are disloyal and betraying the pathogenic parent if they have a relationship with the targeted parent. Words are only 30% of communication. It doesn't matter if the pathogenic parent says, "I want you to have the best relationship with the other parent" (because the textbook says it is child abuse to discourage a relationship with their parents). VIBES DON'T LIE. If the pathogenic parent carries "I don't want anything to do with your parent, I don't trust your parent" in their vibrational field, that is the true message that the kids are receiving. For more support on Parental alienation, look up "Alliance to solve Parental Alienation" and "the Chosen Parent Collective" by Dorcy Pruter.

But of course, I understand John's monster because I have the same monster in me!

FORGIVING OURSELVES IS THE HARDEST!

I didn't find closure until I realized that all the suffering from the marriage and divorce came from me not seeing the truth about him and me. I can never give him what he wants. He can never give me what I want. I was blind and delusional about how *incompatible* we were, all because I was too attached to the *status* of being married. It was me that abandoned myself and silenced myself all these years.

Forgiving myself is hard. I don't know if I can ever get there. I wish I could give you a magic wand to help us forgive ourselves. Maybe I will write a whole book on my many lessons from forgiveness, but below I will attempt at sharing an executive summary of what has helped me the most:

• In a course I took from Dr. Raven Lee, Mary Magdalene teaches there is no sin. The only sin is missing the mark of not knowing our connection with God.

• In a course I took with Master Rulin Xiu, she teaches that the only thing we ever have to apologize for is "not knowing how much we are loved."

• "Everything that is wrong with you began as a survival mechanism in childhood." Gabor Mate.

• Once I saw how every way I acted was just a trauma response, it was easier to forgive myself.

• There is God in all. There is God in John. There is God in me. There is perfection in everyone and everything that happens. Trust the divine process.

That being said, I want to tell you a story about me *pretending* that I have forgiven myself. :)

So two months after the divorce, I went to Sedona. I normally don't have insomnia. But on the last night of my trip, I had anxiety so bad that no matter what healing or mantra I tried, I just couldn't calm myself down. I called a friend for distance healing, and I couldn't even relax enough to receive it. Finally, I asked my spirit team for a message, and I was told that I had been "spiritually bypassing," avoiding looking at all the ways I hate myself and all the things I regret doing. So I coached myself, "Okay, let's do it. You got this!" and I closed my eyes and sentence after sentence, with real tears, I energetically screamed, "I hate myself for doing... I hate myself for saying ... I deeply regret doing.... I deeply regret saying ...." This went on and on until I ran out of things to hate myself for and regret about. Then I found peace and fell asleep. I needed to validate all the things I hated myself for and regretted. I needed to witness and experience all the ways I have wronged myself and my loved ones.

Calligraphy is for diagnosis and is for treatment. It was not until I found some forgiveness for myself that I was able to write the 大寬恕 "Greatest Forgiveness" calligraphy.

EMBRACING ANGER AS A GIFT

Beneath anger is all kinds of grief, shame, and fear—all the shadows that we don't really want to face. Sometimes we are so protective we can't feel anything but anger. The reason why John yelled so much was that he was protecting himself from feeling all his wounds from childhood. If you are a yeller, I invite you to see the anger as a gift.

The gift of anger is that it is a fire that burns upwards. It is a powerful energy that we can use to protect and defend when we are under attack. Anger sometimes arises before we even know why—cultivate this sacred relationship with anger because when we listen to our anger, we will know where our boundaries are. Anger is like a radar of where we have the potential of being violated. The key is to allow the anger to rise and fall like a wave crashing onto the shore. As the anger arises, breathe into the anger and see what is the anger communicating? Then release and let it go. With practice, we can experience the coming and going of anger in about 90 seconds.

Exercise: write a letter to yourself about everything you can't stand and hate. Then apply Byron Katie's "flip it around" method to see how it was actually you that you can't stand and hate.

Suggested music: "Let me love you" by DJ Snake + Justin Bieber

---

Hello. This is the voice of my anger.

You know that abandoning me would mess me up, and you do it anyway. You know you are the most important person in my life, but you choose to give up on me anyways. You know that I have been crying in bed for weeks, and you walk out on me when I need you the most. There is no greater injury than being given up by choice. I don't know what is more painful than shutting me out. How can you close your heart to me after all these years? Do you know it feels like you stabbed me with a dagger in my heart? Do you know my heart is bleeding?

AAAAAAAGGGGGGGGGHHHHHHHHHHH

Ah! Ah! Ah! Ah! Ah! Ah! Ah! (Scream rhythmically to express my anger. Using my body as a drum and allowing myself to enter into a trance to access my anger below the surface...)

It is me. I am the one who has abandoned myself, knowing how much it hurts to split my soul and endure soul loss. I am the most important person in my life, yet I choose to give up on my power anyways. I know that I have been through some dark times, and it is me that kept walking out on myself and not standing up for my truth. There is nothing that hurts more than not being able to stand myself, hating myself, and attacking myself, but I do it anyway. I don't know what is more painful than shutting my higher self out? How can I close my heart and not love myself? Do I know how much I long to be loved by myself? Why can't I just receive all of me—no matter what?

<breathe>

I am so sorry for all the rage I created for myself. Thank you for seeing that I am the person who has hurt and abused me more than anyone else. Can I please stop being a bully to myself now?

I deeply apologize for not knowing how much I am loved. I deeply apologize for all the suffering I caused myself by holding on instead of letting go.

Will you forgive me? I have done my best.

Me.

Now it's your turn! Post your letter on Instagram and tag @HonoringDarkness or post on the free Honoring Darkness Facebook group to share your story in community! #HonoringDarkness #GreatestRage #ShadowWork

For a 90 minute workshop to help process this shadow, check out the 12/08/21 episode "Forgiveness—especially self-forgiveness". Our mind is the one that generates feelings of shame, fear, anger, unworthiness—all kinds of suffering. When we practice forgiveness, we find freedom. Turn our enemy (our mind) into our friend.

https://fb.watch/an34wZ6M6o/
https://mindfulhealingheart.com/circles

2.3

SHADOW OF COMPASSION: NOT LISTENING, UNDERSTANDING, AND ACCEPTING OF SELF AND OTHERS

Compassion is our ability to see, hear, understand, accept, and receive the totality of what the experience the other person is sharing with us. The opposite of compassion is when we hear the other person with our brain but not receive them with our hearts.

I grew up listening to my parents fight—a lot. On any particular car ride or dinner, my mom would do all the talking. My dad didn't speak much because anything he said would be attacked and taken apart by my mom. My brother nor I spoke much either. This is partially why I didn't grow up with a relationship with my dad or my brother. Nobody talked except my mom. She had an anxious attachment style, which made everybody else an avoidant.

My mom was negative and critical about everything, especially complaining about my dad. "You never… I always…" He was always the bad guy, and she was always the victim. I was asked to be the judge and take her side, to be her listener, her therapist, her analyzer. She loved to ask me, "what do you think" and "what would you do" making me take on her pain as my own. My mom thought about all the possible negative scenarios, and she taught me how to fear, how to judge, how to criticize, how to shame, and how to take people down with my words with toxic femininity.

And I did exactly that to John and my kids.

It's funny because growing up, I swore to myself that I would never do to my husband or my kids what my mother did to me. But that is how ancestral karma gets passed down from one generation to the next.

Many years later, way after my awakening, I found out that when my grandmother escaped as a refugee from China to Hong Kong, my great-grandmother did not address her daughter's problems with compassion.

I can think of the countless things my mom said to me that were the opposite of compassion. I can also think of the countless things I said to my daughters that were the opposite of compassion. Years ago, my daughter was frustrated with something and came to me. Instead of validating her feelings, I told her, "you should be grateful," and went on and on about her having a roof over her head, parents that loved her, never having to worry about having enough money to pay for clothes, food, and toys, etc. Another time, a mother texted me about my daughter bullying her daughter at school. Instead of listening to my daughter's story and taking her side, I was too caught up worrying about *my* image and how others would judge *me* as a bad mom who didn't teach her daughter about manners and decency. I was worried about this being escalated to the teachers and the school principal's office. I was worried about my daughter being kicked out of school. I was worried about *me* looking bad. I talked over my daughter instead of listening to her. How my parents didn't show up for me and broke my heart is how I didn't show up for my kids and broke their hearts...

Now that I have more awareness, I can parent with more consciousness. One time my daughter put a cup of tea on the floor instead of the coffee table, and someone knocked it over, and the tea spilled all over the carpet. My first thought was, "I need to teach my daughter a lesson on how to be careful, so she doesn't spill next time! Should I make her clean up with remorse so that she will not repeat the same mistake?" With curiosity, I received my shadow with an internal smile. "Okay, I see you are parenting from unhealed childhood wounds." How would I parent from unconditional compassion? "How can I serve her? Can I help with cleaning? Let me observe her and be present with her to make sure she is okay. If she feels ashamed, I can comfort her until she learns how to self-soothe. I can reassure her that everyone spills tea on the carpet sometimes, and it is absolutely okay to spill." My ancestral karma is to be *harsh* in parenting and use fear/shame/guilt to teach lessons. Can I find compassion for my lineage, myself, and encourage my children to find compassion for themselves?

WHERE DID IT GO WRONG?

When my grandmother invalidated my mom, my mom learned that what she had to say didn't matter. Then my mom grew up feeling unworthy, and she was constantly people-pleasing to seek validation from her husband and her kids. Because she learned that she didn't matter, she constantly _denied_ her own voice and her own needs and gave to others what she didn't have. She didn't love herself and what she gave to her kids was guilt-laden bargaining. "Look at all these sacrifices I made for you. If you don't listen to me, you are a bad person." "I always do all this for you, but you never see me, honor me, or appreciate me." Nothing I did was ever good enough for her because nothing *she* did was ever good enough for her.

Funny because that is exactly my daughter's complaints of me: that she feels like she doesn't matter. Perhaps my lack of relationship with my daughters is not so much because of the parental alienation (of course, it is easier to blame John than to take responsibility for my own shadow), but that up until my awakening, I had been raising my daughters without being willing to step into their shoes and experience their reality. I *invalidated, doubted, not trusted, not received* their words as true. I even *projected* my own meanness and manipulation onto my daughter and assumed that she was mean and manipulative.

WHEN PARENTS INVALIDATE THEIR CHILDREN

- "You're wrong."

- "I know better, and you need to listen to me."

- "You don't know right now because you are young, but one day when you grow older, you will see that I am right."

- "You should feel grateful instead of frustrated."

Children learn that they don't matter, they feel unworthy, and they disconnect from their essence.

The cost of invalidating our children is they stop trusting, expressing, and listening to themselves.

Because I grew up listening to my parents instead of listening to myself, after the rape and the verbal abuse happened, when my perpetrators made excuses and defended themselves—"Oh that was not verbal abuse, that was not yelling, you are just "too sensitive" or "Oh I thought you wanted to have sex." I allowed them to invalidate my experience. Because I had stopped trusting, expressing, and listening to myself—I began to suppress my anger. "Maybe I was too sensitive. Maybe he didn't yell. Maybe that was my imagination. Maybe I remembered wrong. Maybe it's not his fault. Maybe it's my fault." "Maybe I was sending mixed signals. Maybe it was my fault that I got raped. Maybe I shouldn't be mad at him. Maybe he is a nice guy after all." "Maybe I should trust him more than I trust myself."

I am not sure if they gaslit me or I gaslit myself. "Did they hurt me? Did I make that up?"

A people pleaser avoids conflicts at all costs, even at the cost of denying her own experience, so that everything can stay the same and we can avoid facing what happened. By choosing to protect them and excusing their behavior, I was hurting myself, living with more shame, and having more difficulty loving and forgiving myself. It was not until writing this book that I realized I had endured a soul loss. Due to survival, codependency, and people-pleasing ways, I had denied my own trauma and locked my inner child into a closet.

My truth was easily tampered with, and many days I didn't have clarity. I lived in a fog, and men took advantage of my fog. They talked me into thinking I was a victim and needed their rescuing. Their ego wanted to be fed to feel like the knight in shining armor. They gave me help with the intent of conquering me as prey. The guys who believed they were "nice guys" were the most dangerous. They live in a lie. When they don't own their darkness, men manipulate and disarm women into trusting men over trusting themselves. (Women who think they are nice, caring, and nurturing are also dangerous, as they get resentful or even judge others harshly when others aren't nice, caring and nurturing.) "Men are assholes" is a conversation that is perhaps a part of my ancestral lineage and in the collective wounded feminine. In a shamanic session with Jay, a soul retrieval was performed where I had to validate my trauma to awaken the part of me that I had put to sleep. (I don't mean to sound like a salesperson, but there are a LOT of modalities beyond the traditional psychotherapy that are absolutely critical in healing trauma and reconnecting to our original wholeness. I love being a "GP" energy healer who screens people and refers them to other specialists. The field of energy healing is huge. If you are looking for healing, shoot me an email and let me refer you to someone who can help you. If you are a healer and want more business, tell me your life story so that I can refer clients to you. I love making connections!)

RECOVERING MY ABILITY TO LISTEN WITH COMPASSION

Teal Swan says all relationship fractures are due to "the person who is in less pain is not willing to step into the reality of the person with more pain."

When my daughter told me, "You never listen to me," I couldn't accept her perception of me. The people-pleaser in me cannot accept myself as a bad mom. I couldn't accept her experience of me because I couldn't accept my shadows. How I accept myself, including all my shadows, is how I am able to accept my children with all their shadows.

True compassion is to give up justice. To give up judgment. To give up who is right. True compassion is an unconditional acceptance of the other person's reality. Do we want to punish the person who abused us? Seeking justice is like giving pain to the person who gave us pain. It doesn't actually lessen our pain. What actually lessens our pain is mercy.

> "Shame makes little hearts hurt. The heart hardens to feel less to hurt less. The less we feel, the less we care. The less we care, the more disconnected from ourselves and others we feel." - Lelia Schott @Synergy.Parenting

---

My mom has been harsh with me. I have been harsh with me. I have been harsh with my daughters. **How I give up punishing and seeking justice on others is how I give up punishing and seeking justice on myself.** I don't want to live in shame or guilt for myself. Why would I want shame and guilt for others?

SELF-COMPASSION IS THE HARDEST!

Have you ever *resisted* listening to yourself? Here are some examples of me not listening to myself:

- I am tired, but I don't take a nap or go to sleep because the righteous in me wants to get more done.

- I am hungry, but I don't satisfy my craving because the perfectionist in me wants to look like a swimsuit model.

- I am itchy, but instead of meditating on what message is behind the itch, I scratch it so that the pain can numb out the itch.

- My therapist / coach / trainer tells me we are working on our "mother wounds" or our "wounded child" and I groan, "not again! Haven't I done enough work already? Why am I here again?"

- I can't find my cell phone, and instead of finding compassion for the stress I am under, I question, "why are you so dumb, sloppy, all over the place?"

- When my daughter cries because of something I said, instead of finding compassion that I am already doing my best, I trash myself, "why are you such a bad mother? What's wrong with you?"

EMBRACING THE GIFT OF BLOCKING / NOT RECEIVING

Sometimes the totality of the truth is too much. We are simply not ready to receive and digest it. It would be better to block and survive the present moment and return to this later. Sometimes we know what the "right thing" is to do, but we simply don't have the resources to. For example, we know the "right thing" is to listen to our kids, but we simply don't have the time or energy to, and we get to embrace "we got to do, what we got to do." Sometimes the trauma is too much and taking medication to block out some of the self-harming thoughts is better than receiving all the self-harming thoughts. Embrace and appreciate that whenever we block or choose not to receive, it is part of the Tao.

GRIEF IS NECESSARY TO CULTIVATE COMPASSION?!?!

The Chinese word for compassion is 慈悲. The first character is composed of 兹 (zi_1), which means "now, here, this," and 心 (Xin) which means heart. When our heart is in the "here and now," our nature is 慈 (ci_2) kindness.

The second character is composed of 非 (fei_1), which means "not" and 心 (xin), which means heart. When we are not in our heart, we experience 悲 (bei_1) which means sad, sorrow, grief.

Putting the two characters together, we develop compassion when combining kindness and grief. A person with the most authentic compassion is one who has experienced tremendous grief 悲 and, therefore, can empathize with the human suffering and offer kindness and mercy 慈.

Exercise: write a letter to ourselves about everything we feel has been suppressed. Then apply Byron Katie's "flip it around" method to see how I was the one who has been suppressing myself.

Suggested music: "Unsteady" by X Ambassadors

———

Hello. This is the voice of my inner child that has been suppressed and invalidated.

Why can't you ever see me, hear me, or understand me? Why can't you ever open yourself to receive me? Why can't you see things from my perspective? Why can't you find compassion for me? Can't you see that I am already doing my best? Why can't you ever take my side and stand with me?

It is me. It is me that doesn't know me. It is me that doesn't ever take my side because I am too busy doing what makes me look good according to society's arbitrary definitions. It is me that is not open to the perfection that God made me. It is me that can't respect and appreciate my perspective. It is me that can't find compassion for myself when I have already done my best.

<breathe>

It's okay for things not to go the way I want.

It's okay if I don't live up to my kids' expectations of the perfect mom.

It's okay if I had not been able to show up for myself or my kids when they needed me most.

It's okay if my kids push me away or if I retreat to the solitude of my bedroom.

It's okay if my kids are rude to me or if I invalidate them.

It's okay if my kids are mean to me or if I make them do something they don't want, like putting the screens away.

It's okay no matter how badly my kids behave or I behave.

It's okay if my kids or I get mad.

It's okay if I feel that my kids or I hate me right now.

It's okay if my kids or I feel unsafe with our big feelings.

It's okay if my kids or I get defensive.

It's okay if my kids or I avoid vulnerability or intimacy.

It's okay if my kids or I are in denial and are not ready for therapy.

I trust everything happens in divine timing. I am so sorry for all the times I suppressed my voice and didn't listen with compassion.

It's okay to not be okay.

Me.

Now it's your turn! Post your letter on Instagram and tag @HonoringDarkness or post on the free Honoring Darkness Facebook group to share your story in community! #HonoringDarkness #GreatestSuppression #GreatestInvalidation #ShadowWork

When I need divine compassion, I listen to the following:

"Prayer Of St. Francis" by Robert Kochis

- Seek not to be understood, but to understand

- Seek not for others to have compassion for our suffering but to have compassion for their suffering.

"Da Bei Zhou" by Dr. & Master Zhi Gang Sha

- This is the Greatest Compassion Mantra

2.4

SHADOW OF LIGHT: FEAR AND DOUBTS

One of the things I always tell my clients when it comes to compassion for our traumas is that *nobody, not even the best therapist,* can truly validate our pain besides ourselves because nobody else can truly understand what it is to be in your body at any given time. I don't know how anyone in the world will understand the depth and 100% all-in committed love I have for John. How can a woman who has opened her heart to other men still be considered all-in committed to loving a man?

Believe it or not, loyalty + commitment + integrity is something that has always been of critical importance to me. Never had I imagined I would have affairs, but even to this day, I am always considerate of John's needs and try to give him everything I can. After I told him about the affairs in late October 2020, that first Black Friday, I purchased my own bedding. He loved it so much that for Christmas, I gave the new bedding I bought for myself to him, and I slept with an old TV blanket I purchased years ago. At that point, he had already announced to our children that we were getting divorced, and I was already alienated from my children, but I still wanted to give him the very best of everything I had, the way I always saved the best part for my family.

We each have our own unique light, our own unique love language. We each have our own all-in commitment to love. For example, I am all-in committed to loving him no matter what he does to me. I am all-in committed to forgiving him, receiving him, seeing his light, bringing harmony to the family, expressing my gratitude, and saying yes to his requests whenever possible. If he were to lose his legs or eyesight, I would still want to take care of him with my last dying breath. Even though he has divorced me and blocked communications with me, I am still all-in loving him, as my best friend, as my brother, and in whatever capacity he is willing to receive my love.

After the divorce, I would still affectionately tell our children about all the happy memories I had with their dad and all the qualities I appreciate him. I am very protective of my children's relationship with their dad. In the Four Agreements[1], the first agreement is to be impeccable with our words. For me, I was vigilant in being impeccable with my vibrations, especially around my kids, so they only feel the heart-opening true love I have for their dad.

The truth is, the affairs that followed the initial rape *destroyed my trust in myself*. In Chinese, we have an expression 一諾千金 (Yi nuo qian Jin)—it means that one promise is worth thousands of gold. If you have watched Mulan, you know my culture is all about honor. In the old days, Chinese women committed suicide after they were raped to preserve their honor. The rape and the affairs that followed plunged me into the shadows of lost souls. I forgot who I was, what was important to me—**I lost my light**. When I was raped, it wasn't just my body that was taken from me. My light was also taken.

I gave myself 24 hours to cry after the rape, and then I pretended nothing happened. I tried to be strong and held all of it together for my role in the family.

THE TRAUMA RESPONSES, BEFORE AND AFTER THE RAPE

During the 3.5 year affair with the person who raped me, he would frequently tell me that John was gaslighting me. It was not until I wrote this book that I discovered that he was the one that was gaslighting me. I had a classic case of Stockholm syndrome when I developed love, sympathy, empathy, and a desire to protect my violator. Now I see that the reason I "manifested" a rape and continued a relationship with him was that *fawning* was a trauma response in my vibrational field: people-pleasing, lacking identity, needing direction, and codependency.

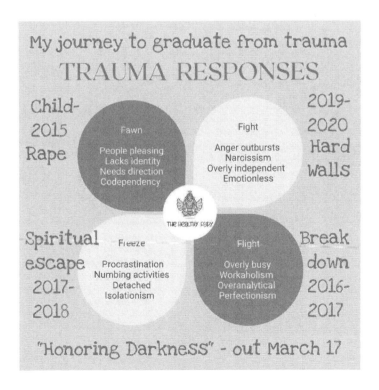

(Dear readers, if you have children, please make sure they are not obedient, not people pleasing, know exactly what they want, and fight for themselves. Raising children who follow the rules and allow parents or authority to suppress their voice or bend their truth increases our children's chances of being verbally, emotionally, or sexually abused. All three of which I have been a victim of. I am so proud to have daughters who have no problems saying "No" to me, throwing their anger at me when we fight, because how they say "No" to their mom is how they will say "No" to perpetrators when they grow up.)

A few months after the rape in 2015, I signed myself up for a four-year Master's degree in Oriental Medicine. On the surface, I was learning acupuncture to help all the chronic physical pain that I dealt with on a daily basis. Below the surface, I relied on being an *overly busy workaholic* as a coping mechanism to run away from my traumas. Of course, that is not a sustainable model, so in 2017 I had a nervous breakdown. When I discovered meditation, I frequently avoided human interaction. I kept myself *detached* and *isolated* as I escaped to spiritual practices. As I learned about boundaries and gained my voice, I set hard boundaries "Oh I won't let anyone take advantage of me anymore," and my unwillingness to compromise about anything ultimately led to the divorce. The submissive Asian girlfriend at 22 morphed into an argumentative fight about everything and won't compromise on anything kind of wife. I "forgave" you for hurting me, but "I am so not going to trust you anymore. I am so not going to let you hurt me anymore. I am so not going to let you talk me out of my position. My boundaries are really firm, I won't let anyone cross my boundaries, and I won't soften."

THE DARKNESS AND FEAR THAT FOLLOWED THE RAPE

When I descended into the world of darkness, I saw the world through the filter of fear and the potential to get more hurt. Years later, when I confessed to John about the affairs, he told me, "I have compassion for your suffering. I wish you had come to me after the rape." But no, I couldn't have. I know he has a gun. I know what finding out someone has raped your best friend / wife would do to him. He already had anger issues, and I was already afraid of his anger. What if he tried to kill or destroy this man? What if this man fought back and hurt John? What if one of them goes to jail or dies because of me? What would happen to our children or the rapist's children?

Looking back, I now see with more clarity that what I used to blame John for (that his yelling caused me PTSD, including shaking, panicking, palpitations, and shortness of breath) was actually caused by my own fears. I was scared that my secrets would be discovered and that those revelations could potentially break our families.

DOUBTING AND LOSING TRUST IN MYSELF AND EVERYTHING

When I confessed about my affairs, John said, "I don't know if I can ever trust you again." I descended further into the darkness. He was my best friend and my rock—for 19 years, I hung on to his every word.

I don't know if I can be trusted after what happened.

I wanted to trust myself so desperately, but his lack of faith in me was like a negative virus that took over my vibrational field. I started doubting, underestimating, and contradicting myself. I went through rollercoasters of extreme highs and lows. One voice in me says, "don't believe him! He doesn't trust you because he doesn't trust himself! He doesn't know me because he doesn't know himself!" Another voice in me says, "why would anyone want to trust you, given your track record?"

The reason trust is hard is because we haven't healed from our past wounds. Hurt people hurt people and don't trust because they are afraid to get hurt again.

When I doubt myself, the frequency of the doubt in my vibrational field will invite others to doubt me. Instead of being a victim of "why don't people trust me," I get to work on trusting myself.

THE ROAD TO REGAINING MY TRUST AND THE CLARITY THAT FOLLOWED

I lived in the dark and obscurity until the graduation of my Kundalini Yoga teacher training in October 2020. I was in the presence of my soul brothers and sisters who loved me, supported me, and believed in me. Doing yoga (moving meditation) and chanting mantras as a group is one of the most powerful ways to connect to our inner light. To chant mantras is to bless ourselves and one another, to give our light, and to receive others' light. At the end of the teaching training, I remember finding the courage, strength, and determination to take responsibility for my affairs by telling John the truth. That is one of the bravest things I did for myself. To own my story and step into the light.

Light cannot happen without compassion. Compassion helps us listen to ourselves. From true intimacy with ourselves, the light + protection + strength + penetration + clarity shine through. Light happens after compassion. When I work with a client, I get to gain their trust by receiving all of them with compassion. Without establishing safety and intimacy, the light that penetrates through illusions may be too hard for my client.

To trust myself is to stand in my power and own the clarity my light brings to myself and the world.

But how? To gain clarity on how to trust, I declared the question to the universe and went to bed. I trust the answer will come when I wake up the next morning, and it did:

My guides showed me that my blockages in trust were trapped in the gallbladder channel, in the rib cage of my left side body. My guides told me to dance. Piecing the hints together, I got the answer.

To trust me and to trust others is to trust the Tao / Source / Universe / Creator. It's "Doing, not doing." It's allowing myself to dance with my body fully aligned in oneness with my energy, my mind, my heart, and my soul. It allows the music of the universe to touch me, move me, and inspire me so that one cannot separate the dancer from the dance.

人法地，地法天，天法道，道法自然. In Tao Te Ching, there is a saying, "Human follows earth, earth follows heaven, heaven follows Tao, Tao follows nature." Therefore, "follow nature's way" and trust the process. Please note: following nature's way is not just *passively* going with the flow of the universe, taking no action, and hoping that things will fall from the sky.

Master Sha teaches 天人各半, which means heaven 50%, human effort 50%. To follow nature's way is to acknowledge 我在道光中，道光在我中: that I am in the source light, and the source light is in me. When we allow ourselves to be nourished by the source light all around us, we will connect to the source light within us, and we will see that we are co-creators. We learn to read signs. We learn to trust our intuition, gut feelings, and spiritual channels. When John asked for a divorce, he said, "God speaks to me and through me too," and I knew he was right. I trust the *guidance* of my source light and the source light that is in John and my kids.

Clairvoyance is the ability to see messages visually. Clairaudience is the ability to hear guidance. Clairsentience is the ability to feel messages in our bodies. Therefore, observe the sensations and feelings in the body. Observe the grief, anger, suppression, fears—this is part of our clairsentient channel. Observe every voice—not just the voice of our mind, but the voice of our heart, our liver, our kidney, our shoulders, our solar plexus, our pelvis, our knees, and our ankles. Yes! Observe every visual sign, such as a rash, a pimple, the eyes, the ears, the tongue. (TCM has a whole system with ear diagnosis and tongue diagnosis—buy a book or take a class to further your own body). Our body is sacred and constantly gives us messages to guide, redirect and protect us. Are we aware? Receive the message, acknowledge, appreciate and then let it go.

Master Francisco Quintero, lead master teacher at the Tao Academy, says when we practice Oneness, we can fully open all the spiritual channels. I honor John's channel as much as I honor my channel.

TRUSTING TAKES PRACTICE

> "The opposite of anxiety isn't calm. It's self-trust." - Tory Eletto of the Imperfect Person Podcast @nytherapist

A bird can hang out peacefully on the branch of a tree, not because it trusts the branch not to break, but because it trusts its ability to fly. We don't go through life hoping nothing will break, but we trust that we already have everything we need inside.

How can we trust our ability to cope with life's triggers when things don't go our way? We get to parent ourselves and be the parents we wish we had. Daniel Siegel and Tina Bryson talk about the "4 S" in their book *"The Power of Showing Up: How Parental Presence Shapes Who Our Kids Become and How Their Brains Get Wired"*[2]:

Safe - We don't judge, shame, punish ourselves so we are emotionally safe and we can turn inwards to the refuge of our heart

Seen - We validate ourselves

Soothe - We offer compassion to ourselves

Secure - When we consistently practice safe + seen + and soothed

Strongly recommend you read this book to cultivate trust, my friends! There is a way through every block, and we already have everything we need inside to succeed.

THE GIFT OF FEAR

Fear is a gift because it protects us from getting hurt. I am so grateful for my fear and the way I protected John from the trauma until I was stronger and more grounded. Years later, I had a client who had depression. When she was in high school, she slept with her high school teacher. When the news came out, the high school teacher killed himself. The teacher's young daughter was devastated, and my client lived with the shame of having caused suffering to his daughter. I don't know if my rapist will ever appreciate me protecting him and his kids. I don't know if John will ever appreciate me protecting him and our kids. But my fear of the consequences of letting the secret out at that time protected everyone.

If I could go back in time, I would have gone to a therapist who does shadow work (and hired someone like Ji or me). But I would still choose to keep the rape a secret from John and the kids. While it was incredibly lonely not to feel understood by my family, it was the most loving gift I made to protect my family.

In Tao Te Ching Ch 25, there's a line: "Humans are great. Mother Earth is great. Heaven is great. The Tao is great." 人大地大天大道大. My point in sharing this story is to illustrate that the Tao is infinite. There are infinite perspectives. Some people believe in seeking justice after a rape. Great! Some people believe in finding forgiveness and compassion after a rape. Great! We are all great! Light is a gift. Shadow is also a gift. Everything that is in the Tao is great. Everything that happened was meant to be that way. My way was to protect my family from my shadow by keeping them in the dark. It's like a tree providing shade at a time when the heat would have hurt them. Your way is going to look different than mine, and that's great!!!

Exercise: write a letter to ourselves about everything we fear. And then delete all the conversations that protected us yesterday but are weighing us down today.

Suggested music: "Losing my way" by Justin Timberlake.

Hello. This is the voice of my doubts and fears.

Beneath the grief of rejection from my daughters, or the anger of being abandoned by John, or the silencing of my pain, is the deepest fear of being stuck in my suffering—that I can never graduate from being a victim. That my daughters would be psychologically scarred by what I have said and done as an unconscious unhealed mom and need therapy the rest of their life, that they will suffer forever. I am afraid that the divorce will damage my children's world, to feel less than their friends who have the picture-perfect family, to look on social media accounts every Thanksgiving and Christmas, and be jealous of the happy family that so many of her friends have. I fear they may be stuck in the dark tunnel and never see the light.

I don't know if I have what it takes to live up to my soul's purpose.

I don't know if I have the discipline to tough it out.

I don't know if I know how to find the balance between doing and being.

I don't know if I am worthy of love after the truth comes out about me.

I don't know if I can ever get better with my chronic physical handicap.

I don't know if I should work harder or let go.

I am scared that I will fail. I am scared of being unsupported.

<breathe>

I am so sorry for all the times I doubted myself and created all these fears. I now see them as illusions that my ego has created for me. Fear is living in the future and not the reality of the present moment.

I now know that there are no mistakes, but just choices I make. Turn left, I go to the beach. Turn right, I go to the forest. Who is to say that going to the beach is better or worse than going to the forest?

I now know that my children have divine light in them and that the best way to guide them is to stay connected to my divine light.

I now know that I am never alone. The universe is always guiding me and protecting me.

I now know that fear is a helpful message that alerts us of potential danger. Once we have received the message, we can let it go and not let fear hold us back from being in the now.

"When the time is on you, start, and the pressure will be off." - Yogi Bhajan.

Let me be guided by my inner light,

Me.

Now it's your turn! Post your letter on Instagram and tag @HoneringDarkness or post on the free Honoring Darkness Facebook group to share your story in community! #HonoringDarkness #GreatestFear #ShadowWork

Ready to process your fears? Watch the 11/17/21 episode on "Overcoming fear, letting go of excuses and harsh control freak" and do the Kriya for state of mind and overcoming paranoia. https://fb.watch/an3jre0e6i/

1. Ruiz, Miguel. *The Four Agreements: A Practical Guide to Personal Freedom.* Amber-Allen Publishing, 2017.
2. Siegel, Daniel J, and Tina P. Bryson. The Power of Showing Up: How Parental Presence Shapes Who Our Kids Become and How Their Brains Get Wired. , 2020. Print.

2.5

SHADOW OF HUMILITY: EGO, ARROGANCE, UNWORTHINESS, JUDGMENT, COMPETITION, AND COMPARISON

At this point in the story, you are probably wondering, how did the rape turn into a 3.5-year affair? How was I served by the affair, and what was so addictive? Why did I put myself in a situation where I could be violated, and why did it take me 3.5 years to ghost him?

When I was 21, my brother called me a "slut" for going to Jamaica on spring break. When I was 24 and wanted to move in with John, my parents called me "damaged goods" because "no man wants a woman who has lived with another man." Fast forward to 35 when the rape happened. Who could I turn to?

"If our children do not believe we are their safe place, they will eventually find safety in something or someone else…"

- Michelle Kenney, M. Ed @PeaceAndParenting

I have already felt unworthy my whole life, and after the rape, I felt like worthless damaged goods. And then the only person whom I felt safe and wanted by was the man who violated me. All humans have attachment needs, and he was the only person I could relax and be myself with. As Gabor Mate would say, "It is impossible to understand addiction without asking what relief the addict finds, or hopes to find, in the drug or the addictive behavior." Before we shame the addict for their addictive behavior, perhaps we can have compassion that the human being was a victim isolated from her parents, siblings, and loved ones, that she feels so alone and so much shame that she couldn't go to anyone for help.

Mr. Intoxicating always listened to me (except when I tried to break up with him). He has seen my worst, and I felt safe around him. He didn't judge me. He didn't yell at me. He didn't tell me what to do. We were both liars and cheaters, and once you have descended to the dark side, it's hard to go back to the light. I felt unworthy, I felt dirty, I felt cheap, I felt that nobody could understand me and I would be rejected by John, the very approval I craved!!! And I was so caught up in my ego about having the "Christmas card perfect" family.

I didn't love myself, and this man did my job for me. And in order for me to stay with Mr. Intoxicating, my mind had to make John into a monster. I labeled his yelling as "verbal abuse" in order to justify why I needed to leave the house. My mind needed to doubt if John ever loved me. My mind created all kinds of illusions. I blamed everything on John in order to not kill myself or hate myself.

When the abortion happened, I went through the entire medical procedure alone. The nurse looked at me and asked if I had anyone for support. I said "No," and she was kind enough to offer me her hand. She told me to squeeze into the hand whenever I felt pain during the procedure, and I was so grateful for that physical touch with another human being, even though that other human was a complete stranger. No woman should ever give birth without a village of love around her, and no woman should ever have an abortion without a village of support either.

No one can validate my shame of rape, abortion, and cheating except for him. Eventually, Mr. Intoxicating became so important to my survival that he was on my "last call list"—I made a promise to him that before I killed myself, I would call him and give him the chance to intervene in my suicide attempt.

If I was John's best friend and John was my best friend, why wasn't John on my "last call list"? Why couldn't I turn to John with my pain? What was wrong with my relationship with John?

TOXIC MASCULINITY AND TOXIC FEMININITY

Growing up, my parents fought a lot. They were the model of codependency. My mom had anxious attachment—she had a negative outlook on everything and worried about everything. (In later chapters, I will share how my mom's over worrying turned into the greatest gift.) My dad was avoidant—he worked hard, he played hard, but he seldom spent time understanding his wife or children. They were the picture of patriarchy. Toxic masculinity, where the man is disconnected from intimacy, feeling and sharing his emotions, and not being able to be vulnerable or able to ask for help. Toxic femininity, where the woman is a helpless, powerless victim, and her only way of getting her way is by nagging, judging, and manipulating with fear, shame, and guilt. The same relationship dynamic was repeated in my marriage. I was a people pleaser, just like my mom. I didn't love myself, and due to the lack of self-care and boundaries, I often felt stressed, fatigued, frustrated, and resentful when I bent myself backward, giving to my husband and my kids but not feeling appreciated or reciprocated by them. Since I didn't love myself, I was constantly seeking approval from my husband and my kids. Perhaps I even made them feel like walking on eggshells because anything they said or did that did not meet my expectations would bring out the moody victim, just like my mom.

John's go-to feeling was anger. My go-to feeling was grief. He did all the yelling, and I did all the crying. I played the victim, and he was **doomed** because he was both the rescuer and the perpetrator. When he was my rock, he was my rescuer. When he yelled, the toxic feminine in me would blame him and shame him for being the perpetrator. Because I was disconnected from my anger (nice girls don't get angry), I didn't have boundaries, and I didn't know how to protect myself. I was dependent on *him* to protect me from *his* anger. Alas. This was a formula for disaster. Every time he got angry, I would be angry at him for getting angry. If I had done the shadow work and owned my anger, I would have compassion for his anger.

Looking back, I don't know if John's yelling was ever that bad. Maybe the real monster was me. Why did my monster come out? Why was I stuck in darkness and not guided by the light within? I didn't trust myself or John, and I couldn't see my light or his light. I saw the world through these filters that kept me trapped in pain. When I was disconnected from my light, I assumed the worst of John.

MEETING THE MURDERER IN ME

About a month after we separated, a girlfriend that I hadn't heard from for over ten years called me out of the blue and asked me, "Are you okay? I saw it on Facebook." What?!?! Due to my shame, I had changed my relationship status to "hidden" for many years. When John changed his Facebook status to "Divorced," the Facebook algorithm automatically flipped my status to divorce to the public.

I was furious. "Does this man have no sensitivity? First, you dump me, discard me on the curb, and you want to pour salt on my wounds by stripping me naked for the world to see?"

I called him and demanded he take down his Facebook status immediately. He didn't reply to my messages for many hours, and I felt like the end of the world was happening. I was pacing in my bedroom and peeing urgently and frequently. I knew my energy was messed up. By 1:45am, I was about to lose my mind, and I saw the third eye image of a knife into a heart. I knew what this meant. I felt like he stabbed my heart with a knife. I knew what I needed to do to survive that moment. I prayed to my guides, "take me to the underworld and guide me back to the light. I will trace hours of forgiveness calligraphy and pray for forgiveness later, but right now, I need to validate my victim and give my anger an expressive outlet."

I put on my music and began a visual meditation where I imagined stabbing John in the heart, over and over again, until my imaginary arm couldn't lift one more time because there was no more anger left in me. And then I drifted off to sleep for two hours.

This exercise was effective. I only had to meet the murderer in me one time, and divine intervention took all the anger out of me. After that, I can never judge anyone for having murdering thoughts. I can never judge anyone for anti-Asian hate crimes. I can never judge anyone anymore. If you have never met the murderer in you, I am so happy for you. Not knowing the murderer doesn't make someone a better person, it just means they are blessed not to have crossed the unbearable pain threshold as a victim yet.

GIVING UP JUDGMENT, COMPETITION, AND COMPARISON

Soon after the divorce, I plunged into the deepest shadow and saw that everything I ever complained about John, my kids, my parents, and everyone else is also in me! I'm every bit as rotten as everybody else. And I have no more light than anyone either. I can finally stop putting others or myself on pedestals.

That really helped me drop judgment, competition, and comparison.

There can be a lot of judgment, competition, and comparison in the healing world. Sometimes western medicine doesn't trust TCM (Traditional Chinese medicine) or thinks that it is inferior as a medicine. Sometimes TCM practitioners say to each other, "my lineage is better than your lineage ."Sometimes healers discredit other modalities, "What I do is scientific and proven. I don't understand why others think spiritual healing can be compared to my medicine." "My modality is better than your modality."

The truth is, we are all One. Yogi Bhajan teaches, "Recognize the other person as me." We are not superior or inferior. Any feelings of unworthiness or arrogance are just an illusion made up by our ego.

EMBRACING THE GIFT OF COMPARISON, COMPETITION, JUDGMENT, AND EGO

The gift of comparison is that it gives us clarity as to *what* we want and *who* we want to be. When we see that another person has what we want—a car, a house, a mate, or a state of mind—we have the opportunity to know our needs and goals better.

The gift of competition is *motivation*. The person we are competing with drives us to do more and do better. Competition can *inspire* us to try harder.

The gift of judgment, whether it is a negative or positive judgment, is it helps us *see* ourselves better. What we like or dislike in another person is what we like or dislike in *ourselves*. We can use judgment as a way to gain clarity.

Each of us has the Shiva of pure consciousness and the Shakti, which manifests abundance from our desires. Therefore, our original soul and our ego are both necessary for seeking purification, fulfillment, and enlightenment. Experiencing pain and pleasure with equanimity instead of resistance is our path being One with the source. Pain is not avoidable, so why not give ourselves permission to experience the totality of pleasure in delicious chocolate, soft fabrics, warm bath, massage, and orgasmic sex? Our ego may desire to look good, to win, to conquer knowledge, to master breath, to open spiritual channels, to get strong in our moving practice (exercise or dancing), to do the right thing, to serve, to be admired by our peers, to be loved by our family, to be appreciated by our clients, to be worshipped by our sexual partner, to have Instagram followers, to have belonging in the community, to be as perfect as possible. Know that all of our ego's desire is part of the perfection of the Tao.

There is nothing wrong with our natural inclination to be a victim, wanting to blame others for everything. That is the gift of judgment—the fear-based ego protects us from getting hurt again. There is nothing wrong with doubting and suspecting either. The ego wants a better life than what we already have. The ego wants to do something to fix the relationships in our lives.

Learn to love, accept and embrace all the gifts of the ego. Our ego is necessary for the physical journey on the human plane. Without the ego, I would not be getting my degrees, writing this book, or teaching acupuncture at a university. We need some greed and some hunger for power to grow. There is nothing wrong with being a righteous perfectionist nerd. I own my ego, I enjoy my personality exactly as it is, and I embrace my story with all my heart.

Exercise: To cut through the illusion, Byron Katie has made the Diamond Sutra accessible to us (please read her books). Let's do an exercise to help us face our hypocrisy by using the "Flip it around method" so that we see that everyone is our mirror. The judgments we inscribe onto others are the judgments we have stamped onto ourselves.

Suggested music: "River Sounds" on Spotify

———

Hello. This is the voice of my ego.

Everything I ever complained about John is in me. Controlling. Reactive. Aggressive. Pushy. Ego-driven. Emotionally unavailable.

Everything I ever complained about my daughters is in me. Shutting down. Pushing love away. Being unreasonable. Scared of the unknown. Numbing themselves with addictive behavior. Not having healthy habits in diet / exercise / sleep.

Everything I ever complained about my mom is in me. Nagging. Shaming. Manipulating. Having her happiness depend on the happiness of her husband and children. Being too judgmental, too critical, too emotional, too all over the place. Name calling. Complaining too much. The way she keeps herself busy to avoid dealing with the real issues.

Everything I ever complained about my dad is in me. Ego. Competitive. Working too hard. Not listening. Not emotionally available. Wanting to look good.

Everything I ever complained about my brother is in me. Not wanting to talk. Wanting to hide and avoid difficult conversations.

Everything that ever drove me crazy about someone, I also do. So instead of blaming others, I take ownership that all darkness is in me. I can stop my arrogance and feel superior to others. That is the work to "recognize the other person as me."

If my kids think that I am not good enough for them, it is because they are not good enough for themselves.

Whatever my kids can't stand about me, it is because they do not love the parts of me that exist within them.

If I am too broken for John, it's because there is so much of himself that he hasn't healed.

If he blames me for hiding and lying, it's because he is hiding and lying from himself and hasn't done the shadow work.

If he feels unsafe around me because I make him feel worthless, it is because he is unsafe with himself, and he makes himself feel worthless.

Everything others complain about me is a reflection of them. I can stop my unworthiness and feeling inferior. That is the work of "recognizing me in the other person."

I am so sorry for all the unworthiness and arrogance that I held on to for too long. Baby bye, bye, bye!

Every time unworthiness and arrogance creep up, it makes me feel better or worse than others. May I be reminded of chapter 66 from Stephen Mitchell's translation of the Tao Te Ching. "Because she competes with no one; no one can compete with her."

Me.

Now it's your turn! Post your letter on Instagram and tag @HonoringDarkness or post on the free Honoring Darkness Facebook group to share your story in community! #HonoringDarkness #FlipItAround #ShadowWork

Ready to give up your resistance to competing and comparing? Watch the 7/7/21 episode of "Inner leader and Inner Follower". Kriya for Liver, Stomach, and colon.

https://fb.watch/7iBvD4loML

2.6

SHADOW OF HARMONY: DRAMA SEEKING AND CONFLICT CREATING

It wasn't the affairs that ended the marriage. I have to give it to John for all the years of psychotherapy he has done. John was an incredibly forgiving and compassionate man. About ten weeks after I told him everything, he was actually willing to let the past be in the past. We briefly reconciled for two months in early 2021 before John declared he was not willing to do the work to keep the marriage going. What happened?

The root cause of the divorce is the power struggle. Due to my unhealed wound, I experienced everything John said from fear and shame and got defensive constantly. And so did he. It became a throwdown of my control freak vs. his control freak. "I must get what I want, this is my baseline, and I won't compromise on my *non-negotiables*" vs. "I can't stay in this relationship unless *you change*." Plus, my anger was suppressed my whole life until June 2020. When I first regained access to my anger, I had a quick temper, and I went from zero to full fire instantaneously. Eventually, the conflict escalating drama queen in me pushed us into a *gridlock* that ultimately led to the demise.

Has anybody wondered, what was the original fracture in the marriage? What destroyed the trust, bond, and connection? It's funny because I have been avoiding telling this part of the story until chapter six because this wound was far deeper than the rape, the abortion, or the verbal abuse.

ORIGINAL BETRAYAL AND WHY TRUST WAS LOST

John and I had the fairy tale beginning. We lived happily ever after. I came from a big family—my dad had eight siblings. I wanted to have a third child, not just because I loved breastfeeding and loved being a mom, but also because I believed that having a third child would give me the opportunity to heal my physical body structurally and functionally—during the birth of my second child, with all the relaxin and epidural in my body, my spine went out of alignment. The organs would sit in the wrong place, and everything that could be in pain was hurting. I had hip pain, lower back pain, shoulder pain, neck pain, knee pain, ankle pain, etc. Because my organs would sit at the wrong place, I would experience stress incontinence, basically peeing all over myself whenever I did any exercise that involved jumping or running. I could no longer exercise and enjoy life like I used to. I experienced chronic physical pain, and I was always cold. Giving birth another time would give me the opportunity to be in the "maximum open" state where structural adjustments and herbs would have the most chance to heal me.

I knew John didn't want another child. He didn't grow up with any siblings. He didn't grow up with a dad. His mom had to work to put food on the table. John was raised by the TV and the bookstore and grew up in isolation. In college, his nickname was "the Wall". Having another child was a lot of work that he didn't want a part of. Eventually, he manipulated me into signing the vasectomy papers. He told me the vasectomy was a way of birth control, the procedure was simple and could be easily reversed. A few months after the procedure, I begged and begged John for another child. "Would you rather see me suffer from chronic pain, day after day, for the next 60 years, than to give me a chance of healing and improving the quality of my life?" He told me, "I have no intention of ever reversing the procedure."

!!!!!!

"If you have no intention of ever reversing the procedure, why did you tell me the procedure was easily reversible? You effectively tricked me into cutting off my fertility so that I can never get pregnant again unless I leave you for another man."

!!!!!!

After that manipulation into signing the papers that effectively robbed my fertility, I never trusted him again. I felt like I always had to watch my back against this heartless man who said he loved me but was willing to watch me suffer in physical pain, day after day, for the rest of my life. Years later, he confessed that he had checked out of the marriage a long time ago. "It's not that I didn't want more children. I just didn't want more children with *you*."

OUCH!!!

That was cruel. He told me the last seven years of the marriage weren't a marriage. That his biggest regret was not leaving me sooner. Two weeks before he dumped me, he was still telling me that he loved me and was my biggest cheerleader. Was that all lies and acting? How can one person go from my biggest cheerleader and that "everything we need can be found in this relationship" to a complete stranger (blocking all communications) in a matter of two weeks?

Either he was a liar and an actor for the last seven years and pretended that he loved me when he didn't, or he said something that he didn't mean. (Because I have certainly said things that I regret and wish I can take back, I am going to assume that John loved me with all his heart and find compassion for his unhealed childhood abandonment wounds that were triggered).

I honestly forgot what our last fight was. During the last two months of our "attempt at reconciliation," he wanted to record all of our conversations. Every time we disagreed, and he raised his voice in anger, he was afraid I would claim verbal abuse against him in court, and he would lose his children. Clearly, affair or no affair, open marriage or closed marriage, none of that mattered because there was no trust in the relationship. He assumed the worst of me, he couldn't trust me, and I haven't trusted him in years either. The scared little boy put up his walls, and the angry little girl did not want to be taken advantage of again. I was afraid that if I put my boundaries down, I am going to lose all of my powers, and I would be easily manipulated and clouded.

Trust creates peace and harmony. When there is no trust, everything turns into conflict.

WHAT WERE SOME OF OUR DIFFERENCES THAT LED TO DISHARMONY?

The pandemic definitely stressed our marriage. John was not comfortable eating outdoors at a restaurant and was angry when I took off my mask to take a photo outdoors at a park. The pandemic triggered his fear and control freak tendency.

Both of us thought the other person needed more therapy. Although he has done years of talk therapy with a psychoanalyst, he doesn't respect the woo woo healing I do that doesn't involve a degree and a license. In his mind, any therapy that is not currently backed by science and textbooks was less legit than the kind that he does. He said, "Winnie, your problem is that you only see the good in people, and you are not willing to look at the ugliness in human nature." He is right that I had been resistant to talk therapy because I carried so much shame that I didn't want to look at all the ways I was wrong, bad, and needed fixing. I wasn't ready at that point to really look at my shadows. For someone with extremely low self-esteem, with suicidal thoughts and addiction, it is helpful to do heart-opening therapies to have sufficient self-love and self-appreciation *before* diving into the shadows.

From my perspective, he hasn't done enough healing from his childhood, and he could really benefit from the heart-opening spiritual healing that transforms karma, etc. Of course, I thought he needed to heal his childhood trauma because *I* needed to heal my childhood trauma!

Basically, both of us were avoiding doing the work it took to make the relationship work. We were both emotionally not available. Neither of us had enough emotional intimacy with ourselves to be able to show up in a harmonious conscious relationship.

DISCOVERING THE UNCONSCIOUS DARK MAGIC / DRAMA QUEEN

I am a firm believer that forgiveness brings freedom. When I first met Raven, she told me my biggest life lesson is to learn to forgive John, that in another lifetime, we were quantumly entangled. He also did something that I was not able to forgive in that lifetime, and that's why I am given another opportunity to practice forgiveness in this lifetime. F*CK, I thought. I better master this forgiveness thing because I so don't want to get hurt again and repeat this lesson over and over.

By the time the divorce happened in March 2021, I had already been a student of forgiveness for years. But forgiveness is not like weight where I can step on a scale and be objectively measured. How do I know how much of the pain John gave me has healed?

In April 2021, I met the murderer in me. In May, I was so mad at him for having my kids hang out with another lady. In June, I thought I found closure. But then September came, and after surrendering myself to the downpour of a waterfall in Big Sur, I met the shadow of my drama queen—my spiritual channel showed me that I was still in so much pain that I secretly wanted him to miss me and regret his choice of dumping me. Wow.

Being an energy healer, I understood that every thought is either a blessing or a curse. Every thought is recorded in the Akashic records. All this time, I was practicing unconscious dark magic. By wishing he would miss me and regret his choices, I was effectively cursing him not to have a happy life. I was at first horrified by my discovery because that's the equivalent of me running a lot of credit card debt to my karmic bank account without my knowing!!! I quickly soothed myself with compassion that hurt people hurt people. I forgave myself for practicing unconscious dark magic, and I reached out to my soul brother Terry Mcgill, a long-time Master Sha student who is excellent at Akashic Records reading.

Pretty much every time I am in a crisis, I book a session with Terry. He advised me to break the patterns of the mind by connecting to the original soul, completely surrendering and receiving the nourishment + protection + support from our original soul to meet all of our needs. He advised me to shift from "what can I get" to "what can I give." Beyond forgiveness, practice *reparation*. I didn't even know what that word meant, so I looked it up. Reparation is the act of making amends for a wrong that was done. At the next circle, I led a metta meditation practice where I sent loving kindness to myself, to my loved ones, and to those who hurt me, such as John. You can do the kriya to relieve inner anger and watch that episode here: https://fb.watch/7VWfvKM7lK/

WHY IS IT SO HARD TO HAVE HARMONY?

We create drama because wounds are sticky. They make it difficult for us to receive, digest, and be nourished by life's experience. Why do I stay mad for the pain someone gave me? Because of spleen dampness. This is tied to the stomach spleen function of transformation and transportation. In Traditional Chinese Medicine, we believe that dairy, deep-fried, greasy or sweet food have a damp, heavy, sticky quality. Dampness is difficult to transform.

Carbohydrate is a double edged sword. In Five Elements theory, each taste has a specific function. Sweet (carbs) soothes, acrid expels, salty softens, sour astringes, and bitter descends. Every molecule we put inside our mouths is medicine! When I am stressed, I sometimes self prescribe carbs to soothe. However, if my body is used to eating carbs, then it develops a tolerance so that I need a large dosage of carbs to be effective. If I have used carbs to soothe for a long period of time, then I may even create imbalance in the body such that my body can no longer process them effectively. Carbs can soothe, but carbs can also increase our resistance and intolerance of life's challenges. The heaviness and stickiness of dampness can make life challenges more difficult for ourselves.

Some of us are blessed and born with a stronger digestion (you can thank your ancestors for good karma). However, if you are like me (empaths that are easily bloated), or you may be habitual over-thinking, have a hard time moving on from the past, worry about everything in the future, attached to certain fixed outcomes... then I strongly recommend you to practice conscious / mindful eating. Before you put anything in your mouth, ask yourself, "Why am I eating this? Do I need soothing right now? Is there any other way besides food that I can use to soothe myself?"

I have chronic dampness problem, so I am most certain I will write another book on this topic as I transform myself!

TURNING THE OTHER CHEEK

In the months of November and December 2021, I practiced tracing and writing Master Sha's Tao Calligraphy of Forgiveness[1]. Then in January 2022, the universe put me to another "spiritual testing". Having done all the work of meeting my shadow, my murderer, my unconscious dark magic drama queen, I was surprised that I learned to turn the other cheek! At one of Master Sha's events, I had the honor of being picked as a demo by Master Sher O'Rourke. She gave me a crown chakra blessing to connect with my most important ancestor, St. Francis. When I connected to the Prayer of St. Francis, I instantly knew why he was showing up to help me at this time. "Seek not to be understood, but to understand. Where there is injury, pardon."

What I realized as the wisdom of turning the other cheek is that hurt people hurt people. What that means is that, whether I offer the other cheek or not, the other person is going to strike again because the perpetrator was first a victim! I have a choice of blocking, returning the strike, or accepting his strike. By connecting to the Prayer of St. Francis like a mantra, I was able to find compassion for John: how lonely he must be, how much pain he must have, to deliver this pain to me. Offering the other cheek *empowers me*. It empowers me to choose my own fate, to claim my action and the accompanying reaction. It keeps my power *with me*. Only light can transform darkness. I get to access my divinity and have the sacred honor of being a trash can. By being aware of and owning my darkness, others' hurtful words and actions no longer trigger me. I can listen to them without taking their hurtful words personally, knowing that what they say is about them, not me. I can receive another's darkness, recycle it, and transform it into unconditional love.

Make no mistake. Turning the other cheek is not easy. It doesn't mean the strike didn't hurt. It means that my faith is so strong that I can dig deep to find the strength and courage to "Let it be." Anything I say or do can be taken as blame or prolonging the drama. I break the cycle by choosing to let it be—"No Response Necessary," as Dorcy Pruter teaches. I choose harmony over conflict. I choose to be a tree that recycles carbon dioxide into oxygen.

EMBRACING THE GIFTS OF CONFLICTS AS OPPORTUNITIES FOR INTIMACY

I used to fear conflicts, but now I appreciate conflicts as opportunities for growth. When people come from different cultures and different traumas, they are going to see things differently. Can we appreciate the richness and the diversity that makes up the vibrant universe? Our perspectives can be different coming from East Coast vs. West Coast, Asian vs. Latin, Buddhist vs. Christians, science vs. spirituality. Oneness happens when we can come together and listen to each other with Differentiation, having intimacy and compassion with another without losing our own truth. Yogi Bhajan says, "Understand through compassion, or you will misunderstand the times."

When I was a kid, I used to hate it when my mom and dad would argue. But now, I see it as a blessing that my mom and dad are so different. The differences make them fight, but it is also the differences that make them a great team, each bringing different gifts to the family.

My dad is a "go with the flow" kind of guy. Being able to trust the process, my dad is naturally relaxed and at ease. He is observant, present, kind, and forgiving. My mom is a "question and worry about everything" kind of person. Being comprehensive in the planning, organizing, defending, providing, protecting, thinking, analyzing, optimizing, attending to every logistical detail, she is able to make things happen and ensure we get the maximum results. Because of their differences, although they fought a lot, they also balanced each other out. Instead of avoiding the triggers, if we find the courage to honor another's perspective without losing our own, we create opportunities for intimacy.

Exercise: write a letter to ourselves about those parts of us that create conflict. And then find a way to integrate the conflict into harmony.

Suggested music: "Before you go" by Lewis Capaldi

Dear the parts of me that are in conflict with one another:

A part of me wants to rest, and a part of me wants to work.

A part of me wants to serve my interests, and another part of me wants to serve others' interests.

My brain is analytical, and my feeling body is emotional.

Sometimes I want to expand and grow; other times, I want to contract and stay safe in comfort and familiarity.

Sometimes I am scared to start a new project.

Sometimes I am scared to walk away from a relationship.

Should I come or should I go?

Should I say yes, or should I say no?

Sometimes it feels like there are so many voices in me that are fighting for resources.

Sometimes I want to be everywhere with everyone.

Sometimes I want to be nowhere with no one.

This morning, I noticed that I wanted to split myself into six: 1) I want to grocery shop and cook a special dinner for my kids; 2) I want to go to yoga and move my body; 3) I want to cuddle someone and feel loved; 4) I want to work on a long term project; 5) I want to get pampered; 6) I want to take a class online to be with my spiritual teacher.

If I don't go grocery shopping, I feel like a bad mom.

If I don't go to yoga, I feel like a lazy person who keeps making excuses why she doesn't exercise.

If I don't make time to cuddle, I fear that my partner will complain that I don't prioritize him.

If I don't work on my long-term project, I fear that none of my long-term visions will come to fruition.

If I don't get pampered, I fear that I am not charging my batteries sufficiently for all the work that I do.

If I don't go to my teacher's online class, I feel like a bad student who is not receiving his wisdom and blessings.

Alas, the voice of fear and shame is creating drama and conflict in my life. I can't be everywhere with everyone all at once.

Instead of feeling guilty and shame that I am a bad student, bad mom, bad friend, bad lover who doesn't take good care of herself...

I am exactly where I need to be. And everyone else is exactly where they need to be, whether they choose to be in my presence or not, whether they choose to receive me or not.

Trust the process! As the peace inside me grows, so does the harmony in my external relationships. My dear, thank you for doing the shadow work of integrating my shadow with my light so that I can trust the process and go with the flow.

May there be peace and harmony,

Me.

Now it's your turn! Post your letter on Instagram and tag @HonoringDarkness or post on the free Honoring Darkness Facebook group to share your story in community! #HonoringDarkness #GreatestConflict #ShadowWork

Ready to process? Watch the 10/20/21 episode "Gain control by surrendering. Surrender by controlling—Yin yang laws.

https://fb.watch/an3rzeGT2f/

---

1. www.DrSha.com

2.7

SHADOW OF FLOURISHING: LACK AND SCARCITY MINDSET

I grew up watching Snow White, Sleeping Beauty, and other love stories with a "damsel in distress." I believed that one day my Prince Charming would come and rescue me. When I met John years ago, I was a needy princess. When John came into my life, he was like a life-saving raft that kept me afloat. When John manipulated me, I felt like a victim. When I was raped, I felt like a victim. When John declared he wanted a divorce, I felt like a victim. When he told the girls that he could never trust me again and the kids alienated me, I felt like a victim. When he played video games and video chat on the nights I had the girls, I felt like a victim.

Pretty much everything made me feel like a victim. When he blocked all communications with me, I felt like a victim. When he failed to communicate, and I showed up to school with no daughter to pick up, I felt like a victim. When I got angry, I felt like a victim. When I hated myself for being trapped as a victim, I felt like a victim.

But it's not just the fairytales that make me a victim. It's also the songs we listen to. The culture I grew up with—the matrix.

HOW PATRIARCHY SUPPRESSED WOMEN AND MEN

The patriarchy suppressed women. Here are some ways:

1. Wearing heels keeps a woman ungrounded. It makes it harder to run away from a perpetrator. Permanently changes the structure of her hips, knees, and ankles. It changes her center of gravity. It creates more curvature to her spine and makes her boobs and ass more attractive but also limits her central channel flow, so she is less connected to her womb power.

2. In my culture, pale skin is desired. By keeping a woman indoors, she is disconnected from yang, from fire, from power. A woman who doesn't get enough sun is also disconnected from God and is more likely to suffer from depression, water retention, and other metabolic issues.

3. Preferring women to look young and look good, so women are obsessed with wrinkle creams, hair products, weight loss, and feeling shame about their body instead of worshiping their bodies and using their bodies as a temple to know God.

Patriarchy also defines masculinity as a man who is strong, who can protect and provide, who can't cry or be weak. Patriarchy essentially forces women into the role of powerless victim and men into the role of powerful rescuer and perpetrator.

THE ROLES OF VICTIM, RESCUER, AND PERPETRATOR IN PARENT-CHILD AND TEACHER-STUDENT RELATIONSHIPS

By choosing to identify as a victim, I make everyone else a rescuer or perpetrator. My parents, John, my therapists, and my teachers became the rescuer and perpetrators. It didn't matter if they were actual rescuers or perpetrators. For as long as I experienced them through my victim filter, every time I was triggered, my trauma response said, "it's their fault."

But I am not always the underdog in a power struggle.

As a parent, when I choose to be a rescuer, I disempower my children and make them into a victim, and then they see me as a perpetrator. For example, my teenage daughter acts like a victim when she doesn't like any of the food I cooked for breakfast and blames me for going to school hungry. I can be a rescuer and try to be a people-pleaser by saying, "What can I make for you," or I can give up my attachments to being liked and empower her to make her own breakfast. I *love* the feeling of being a rescuer. I *love* when my kids used to put me on a pedestal and think highly of me. I *love* being able to protect and provide, but every time I do it, I am essentially robbing my kids of their own power and training them to be victims. It is important for our kids to be independent so that they won't be easily taken advantage of.

As a teacher, my ego *loves being worshiped* and having followers who do things exactly the way I do them. As a healer, my ego loves having clients that come back again and again. Let's be honest, there is no better feeling in the world for my ego!!! But I must resist the urge to be a rescuer if I don't want my students or clients to become powerless victims. In Tao Te Ching Chapter 2, "The master teaches without saying a word." The true meaning is that the master teaches by loving the student, supporting the student, and empowering them to become their own expression of the Tao. Therefore, no verbal instruction is necessary.

The most selfless gift is to help them discover their own gift and encourage them to be their own expression of the Tao, instead of cloning my students to be just like me or having my clients depend on me for healing. In Tao Te Ching Chapter 7, "When the Master governs, the people are hardly aware that he exists. Next best is a leader who is loved." Here is an example. I can bake banana bread, brag about how tasty my banana bread is, and solicit love and appreciation from my daughters for how wonderful it is to have a mother who bakes banana bread. This is the second-tier leader, the kind that is loved. The first-tier leader is one where the children bake their own banana bread (or brownie), and when they are done, they think that they did it themselves. The mother does not take credit for making the money to pay rent, electricity, gas, or bananas. It is the backbone, the foundation, and the structure that the mother puts down that allows her children to flourish. By not taking credit and not needing appreciation, a first-tier master is able to offer true unconditional love.

The best teachers let their students learn from other teachers. Kahlil Gibran says, "If you love somebody, let them go, for if they return, they are always yours. And if they don't, they never were." This non-grasping way of loving and humble service works with romantic relationships, parent-child relationships, and teacher-student relationships. In Tao Te Ching chapter 8, "The supreme good is like water, which nourishes all things without trying to. It is content with the low places that people disdain. In a dwelling, live close to the ground. In governing, don't try to control. In family life, be completely present."

ENDING POWER STRUGGLES

Every time I am triggered in a power struggle, I look at all the ways I identify as a victim and reclaim the power I had given away.

Every time I want to help or give advice that is *unsolicited*, stop. Look at all the ways I identify as a rescuer and give space to our loved ones, children, and students to learn their own lessons and walk their own paths. Encourage them to fly, and let them know how much we appreciate every time they come back to the nest. *Wait* for them to ask for help, and then thank them for giving us the opportunity to serve them!

Another way I can step out of the victim-rescuer-perpetrator roles is by being humble. See that I am as worthy as any man or any teacher, and what I have to share is as wise, insightful, or enlightening as what they share with me. See that I have as much to learn from my children, followers, or clients and truly enjoy listening and receiving their breakthroughs as my lessons as well.

Man and woman, join as One. Parent and child, join as One. Teacher and student, join as One.

FROM VICTIM TO OWNING MY POWER

For years I continued to dwell as a victim. I got really good at sitting in the dark with compassion, but I was not walking myself out of the darkness. It wasn't until I attended Lifeworks Transformation Training with Diana Miranda that I discovered my secret commitment to staying a victim. She helped me delete all the conversations that were holding me back from the person I wanted to BE. Whenever I told Diana stories of being a victim, she would say, "Yes, I hear what you are saying. Do you want to be *right* about being a victim?" Mic drop. No, I don't want to be *right* about being a victim if being right means I *stay* a victim....

At the beginning of the training, my thoughts were, "how can he treat me like this?" Eventually, I shifted that to "How have I given my power away and how can I reclaim my power?" and "How can I share my light with this person?" The program helped me build trust in myself, gain confidence in my integrity, and be "all-in" with how I show up. It is because of this program that I am writing this book.

With great power comes great responsibility. When we say yes to power, responsibility, and leadership, we will no longer feel controlled, suppressed, limited, shamed, emasculated, invalidated, and accused. Our light, strength, and determination will protect us against being blamed, so it doesn't matter what others say about us.

Fierce passion is needed to break through the illusion of victimhood.

Want to graduate from victimhood? Go run in the sun. Cultivate yang. Get your ass off the couch and start doing something.

Want to graduate from being a rescuer / perpetrator? Mind your own business. Stop being so codependent and feeling like it's your job to rescue or fix anyone. Help those who ask for help by empowering them to do it themselves. Give up the ego's attachment to feeling needed, worshiped, admired, and appreciated by those we help. Sit down in solitude and just be a tree that provides shade when others walk up to you. Stop being the people-pleasing nice guy or the nice mom. As Sofia Sundari says, "Nice guys always want something from you." Honestly, it's so hard to let go of my attachment to being a nice mom, but by being a nice mom, everything I do comes with a hidden agenda. I want my love to be reciprocated by my daughters, and that is like giving her a stuffed animal with a knife inside. Being nice brews resentment when the nice gesture is not returned. Even worse is when you shove your niceness into another person's face. When you force someone to take your gift that they don't even want.

WE CREATE OUR OWN REALITY

We see a lot of quotes on social media about "creating our own reality." Is it true, or too good to be true?

Here is one way that I worked through my limiting beliefs and lack mentality.

In the typical aftermath of a divorce, we tend to think about splitting the kids 50/50 as the best scenario. As if our children's love is something finite that we have to fight about. If I operate from a lack mindset, then I would get really petty about how the time is split.

When John plays video games or video chats with our children on my nights, I can operate in a lack mentality and think, "hey, that's *my* time," or "you are *undermining* my parenting," or "you say you support your children having a relationship with their mother, but what do your actions say? Are you encouraging or interfering?"

Or, I can choose to believe that my daughters' love is infinite. The mother-daughter bond is unbreakable. There is nothing in the world that can stop my daughters from loving me unconditionally. My daughters can love my co-parent and me unconditionally, and there is truly no need to hoard. Their love is abundant, and their time can be shared.

GIFT OF LACK

Having money and power is a blessing. It allows us to give. Not having money or power can be a blessing. It gives us the opportunity to ask others for help and service. "Connection is the single biggest need for a physical human" by Teal Swan. Whether we are the one giving or the one receiving, we are serving each other's human needs with the connection.

Nobody has everything in this world. Some people have more money, wisdom, love, health, or support network community. Abundance is something we create by trading with others. What can I give to others, and what can I ask others to give me?

> "There is only one happiness in life, to love and be loved." -George Sand.

Codependence is a win-win or a lose-lose depending on whether both parties practice humility. Teal Swan explains this concept of a transactional relationship that it is important to know what we get from others and what we give to others. Knowing the details of the trade, energy exchange, and transaction is the *foundation* of *conscious relationships* and helps everyone appreciate themselves as a gift and others as a gift. Knowing exactly how we are benefiting from the relationship helps us be in gratitude, to value self, and value others.

For example, even though I am a healer and I have all the coping skills or prayers and meditations and yoga, I have health challenges. Qi deficiency makes me tired easily, cold makes me scared easily (kidney weakness), and dampness makes me more easily stuck in depression and victim. Of course, I take responsibility for taking care of myself with proper diet, exercise, regular acupuncture, yoga meditation, and sleep. Still, I can benefit from being in a transactional relationship with a man who has a lot of yang energy, runs hot, and has great health and strength.

Kids, the elderly, or people with physical handicaps are in codependent relationships. They need someone to provide and protect them. With humility, they can offer a lot of love, gratitude, and opportunities for service.

"THERE IS A WAY THROUGH EVERY BLOCK."

So, life gets hard, and we start doubting if we can be a co-creator. How do we get through it? By knowing who we get to BE, whom we need to comfort, and when we need and ask for help. For example:

- "I am a beautiful, loving, powerful healer goddess-queen-priestess." This is who I get to be when I want to shine and radiate my light with the world.

- "I am a hardworking, people-pleasing, submissive slave victim nerd." This is whom I need to comfort and support with compassion when I sit in the dark with my victim.

- "I am a humble, curious, needy baby that loves to be pampered and taken care of in your arms." This is who I choose to be when I need and ask for help in the physical or spiritual realm. I declare my needs for love and receive with open arms.

The key is to understand that flourishing is a combination of human actions and asking for help. To make things happen, we get to be fierce queens and crying babies! Be completely accountable for our actions, but also ask for help and surrender to all the abundance God gives us.

When life gets hard, ask for help. I like to think about my spirit guides, hanging out, and watching everything happening on earth like a movie being played. When I call on them for help, they jump up in joy, "hooray! I am so excited you called on me to serve you. Serving you is my purpose, and I am so grateful for the opportunity to serve you."

The key to abundance is asking and giving ourselves permission to receive. Ask, and we shall receive. Don't take my word for it. Every time I have been stuck and asked for divine intervention, I receive grace.

PRACTICAL TIPS FOR MAXIMUM FLOURISHING:

• Own your sex. Walk into every room with your entire being, including your genitals.

• Posture, posture, posture! When we sit too much or cross our legs or arms, we physically limit our flow.

• Move. Move the physical body.

• Visualize. My infinity is a carefree, wild woman in nature.

THE GIFT OF LIMITS IS SAFETY

By making my parent, partner, or teacher a rescuer, I disempowered myself. But everything needed to happen exactly the way it happened. I needed my parents, John, and my teachers to be my rescuer before I grew strong enough to flourish on my own.

Every human has safety needs. Own your needs and make sure they are met, either by ourselves or ask for help. Now, I am my best friend, best parent, best coach, and best teacher. I give it to myself *good*—but I also have intimate relationships with others.

Exercise: write a letter to ourselves about our lack and limiting beliefs. Then delete the conversations and give ourselves permission to dare greatly!

Suggested music: if you identify as a victim: "This Town" by Niall Horan

If you identify as a rescuer: "Done for Me" by Charlie Puth

Hello. This is the voice of my lack and limiting beliefs.

I am a powerless victim stuck in my suffering. I can never outgrow my pain.

I feel like no matter how hard I try, I never get what I want. I want to have intimate relationships with my daughters, but I feel powerless. A relationship takes two people, and I can't force them to open their hearts to me. I am never good enough and don't have what it takes to show up as the mom I would like to be.

<breathe>

Keep showing up to do the work, the exercise, and the therapy. Keep the trust, faith, and confidence in myself and that the cosmos will bring healing, reunification, love, and appreciation in divine timing. "Vibrate the cosmos, and the cosmos will clear a path." Yogi Bhajan.

Trust!

Me.

Now it's your turn! Post your letter on Instagram and tag @HonoringDarkness or post on the free Honoring Darkness Facebook group to share your story in community! #HonoringDarkness #LimitingBeliefs #ShadowWork

Ready to expand beyond your limitations? Watch the 11/3/2021 episode "Asking for help" https://fb.watch/an3nDto8mo/

2.8

SHADOW OF GRATITUDE: TAKING EVERYTHING FOR GRANTED

At this point in the book, I want to SCREAM how grateful I am to myself and my spiritual channels and how much joy it has been to reconnect with myself and my channels by writing this book. Even if nobody reads it, writing this book has been a major turning point in my life in discovering how accurate and reliable my channel is. Every morning, my guides would help me gain clarity on my blind spots. What I know I know is 0.0001%. What I know I don't know is 1%. What I don't know I don't know, aka my blind spot, is 99%. I can't believe how lucky I am to have my spiritual channels open and finally be able to trust going inside myself for answers.

I didn't always have this clarity. It took losing my best friend and my rock, hitting absolute rock bottom, to open my spiritual channels. One of the blind spots I was shown is how I had been taking everyone and everything in my life for granted. I never appreciated John enough.

Most importantly, it also took a divorce to realize how everyone and everything has been taking *me* for granted. He never appreciates me enough because I don't appreciate me enough!!!

I highly recommend everyone who is going through or has gone through a divorce to read "Conscious Uncoupling" by Katherine Woodward Thomas. This book is what helped me turn the biggest trauma in my life into the biggest blessing. The stories and exercises in her book helped me discover my source fracture. I went from having the source fracture that "I am not worthy and appreciated" to deeply owning that "I am a gift to the universe."

TURNING TRAUMA INTO A BLESSING

One of my primary complaints about John was that he was always telling me what to do. Mansplaining. He was always trying to fix me, control me, and get me to do what *he* wanted me to do. I felt trapped and not free. He made me feel like a criminal (I later understood it was actually my shame that made me feel like a criminal; however, he tried too hard to fix me and fix the relationship, and "he just kept on pushing my love over the borderline...."). It was his relentless pushing that also brought out the part of me that pushed him over the edge. We were mirroring each other and simultaneously pushing each other over the edge. He may have experienced me as a high conflict individual, but it was his high conflict streak that brought out my high conflict streak. If one of us had cultivated peace, the relationship would not be broken. Every relationship rupture takes TWO. Don't ever take all the responsibility. We were both victims. We were both perpetrators. We both took turns hurting each other with our words.

The biggest blessing was John saying, "I no longer want to participate in the fighting." I was heartbroken to be rejected and to be given up on. That he didn't have enough faith and trust in our friendship to make it work. But in reality, he gave me the biggest gift in declaring he was out. When one person says, "we are no longer going to be in the cycle of hurting each other," it is the hardest thing but also the biggest blessing.

Healing occurs when someone breaks the cycle of fighting. I got to look at the truth that "Yes, it wasn't working." I got to see the truth that I kept pushing, and he kept pushing. I got to see the truth of my attachments, "Why can't I just give up?" He had the opportunity to look at why he gave up so easily. He was scared to face his vulnerability. I was scared to see my worth and that I could thrive on my own, that everything I needed was already inside me.

We had so much love for each other, but both of our unhealed wounds were triggering each other. We needed time apart to grow. To reflect. To see that we were both avoiding our triggers and we both needed a divorce to stop avoiding our source fracture.

It doesn't matter if John does the work or not, because I have already taken the opportunity to look at it. While it takes two people to make a relationship work, it only takes one person to change the dynamics of a relationship. I no longer want to be the victim, rescuer, or perpetrator. I no longer want to create drama. Therefore the relationship will change.

HEALING ONE ASPECT OF LIFE HEALS ALL ASPECTS OF LIFE

It's funny how the source fracture of unworthiness shows up in every relationship in my life. The crisis in one relationship healed my relationship with my parents, my teachers, and myself.

Because of my victim filter, I felt that my parents were always telling me what to do, using fear and shame to coerce me into obedience. I felt like I didn't matter, and I was not listened to.

Because of my victim filter, I would experience my teachers as putting themselves on a pedestal. If they don't know better than I know, then how come they don't make themselves available listening to what I have to say? If they really wanted the best for their students, then why do they put their students through all kinds of testing and put in all these ladders / structures and make their students climb all kinds of Level 1, 2, 3? If they want their students to flourish, then how come they don't encourage us to study with other teachers and make us feel bad for not continuing to study with devotion to only one teacher?

John, my parents, and my teachers were all telling me what to do because they cared deeply about me. They all played the role of rescuer as they didn't want me to suffer. They tried to "teach / fix / improve" me because they wanted to alleviate me from my suffering. Their egos enjoyed being my rescuer. I get them completely because my ego loves being the rescuer too.

FREEDOM VS. STRUCTURE, GROWTH VS. SAFETY AND STABILITY

Because of my unworthiness, because I couldn't see myself as a gift to the universe, I resented all the structures. Yes, structures gave me safety, stability, and support, but I also felt trapped. And I rebelled. Hard. For complete freedom. I didn't want rules. I didn't want discipline. I hated every time someone wanted to talk about boundaries because boundaries meant someone was shutting me out or keeping me small. I hated everything hard, like rules.

At the completion of my LifeWorks training with Diana Miranda, I finally saw that I am a gift to the universe. I was the one who was staying a victim and keeping myself small. Once I loosened my identity as a victim, I began to appreciate the structure that others have been giving me.

> "In the beginning, follow the rules. Then give yourself the space to expand."
>
> -Kooly Totten
>
> Yoga teacher, and Ayurvedic medicine practitioner.

Structure is necessary for freedom and growth. In the beginning, I benefited from the structure that John, my parents, and my teachers gave me. Eventually, I am the only one who can provide the freedom and structure that I need because I know myself better than anyone else. Each of us are on the journey to recover our autonomy and respect for each other. If I give myself freedom and structure, I can honor others' freedom and structure.

As I gained more strength and discipline, I realized how much I love setting boundaries for myself, putting my screens away, going to work out, and creating a safe container for me to sit with my darkness.

> "We can't find safety and connection in relationships until we can first find bravery within ourselves."
>
> -Julie Menanno
>
> Psychotherapist @theSecureRelationship.

I now enjoy all the structure and freedoms in my life. Sometimes I stick to the schedule and go to work. Sometimes I cancel work to go on vacation. Sometimes I turn down a friend's lunch invitation for work. Sometimes I cancel work to have lunch with my friends.

The truth is, we need a container to grow. Yes. Cycling between our finite boundaries and our infinite expressions is part of the Tao. Expansion is followed by contraction—contraction is followed by expansion.

GIFT OF BEING A VICTIM, A RESCUER, AND A PERPETRATOR

The victim, rescuer, and perpetrator are all part of the cycles of the Tao. A perpetrator hurts someone, and a victim is born. The victim gets help from a rescuer. If the victim heals, she wants to be a rescuer to help others. If the victim doesn't heal, her bitterness and resentment turn her into a perpetrator.

The shadow of gratitude (accepting what is as gifts) is complaining (rejecting what is as burdens). What's wrong with my relationship? What's wrong with my childhood? What's wrong with my kids? What's wrong with the way or the amount I exercise? What's wrong with my spiritual practice? What's wrong with my work? What's wrong with my body? The righteous perfectionist in us either wants to be a blaming victim, a fixing rescuer, or a pain-giving perpetrator. The more we are in judgment, the more we pick apart what is wrong, the more firmly we multiply and stay trapped in the dance of the victim rescuer perpetrator cycle. Recognize everyone has the victim, rescuer, and perpetrator inside us. We all like to blame, we all like to fix, and we all know how to fly daggers into our weak spots and tear them down with our words.

It took a divorce for me to finally stop and transcend the cycle of searching for what's wrong, what needs fixing, and "I need you to feel how much pain I am in." Life is full of good and bad as each coin comes with heads and tails. It is our choice if we want to stack our coins and count our blessings or count our misfortunes. What we vibrate is what we manifest...

We transcend the victim rescuer perpetrator cycle when we realize that every trauma is simply a fire that we distill and purify into our true essence. We would not want to leave gold on the table, and we would not want to rob others of their opportunity to dig their own gold.

If it weren't for my spinal injury that caused a pelvic misalignment and that everything that can possibly hurt, hurt, I would not have gone to acupuncture school at 35 and become so good (I can needle myself like I brush teeth). If it weren't for my anxiety, depression, insomnia, and mental breakdown, I wouldn't have had the car accident that led to my spiritual awakening. If it weren't for the divorce, I would not have had many dark nights of the soul, do all the shadow work to see how my shit stinks as much as everybody else's. I would not have come to the realization that I am not superior to those who don't meditate / chant mantras / practice forgiveness, and I am not inferior to my teachers.

When someone gives us pain, welcome every person and every opportunity for coaching us to be stronger.

Exercise: write a letter to ourselves about everything we took for granted and then flip it around to make peace with others taking us for granted.

Suggested music: "(Everything I Do) I do It For You" Bryan Adams

---

Hello. This is the voice of me taking things for granted.

I can never thank my parents enough. They have done so much for me. No matter how many times I have said nasty things to them and broken their hearts, they never stop loving me. They never stop giving me the best of what they got. Food, clothes, shelter. They never stop worrying about me, teaching me, taking care of me, providing for me, and protecting me. I can't believe I used to find all of their love annoying and didn't want to receive their love.

I can never thank my teachers enough—Raven, Master Sha, and countless more teachers in my life. For years, I turned my back from one teacher to the next. I can't believe I used to question and not trust their teachings. Now I receive all of them wholeheartedly.

• I am so blessed to have received psychotherapy and my Integrated Shakti Reiki attunement from the beacon of the divine feminine, Dr. Raven Lee. When I first met her, I was crying twice a day, sometimes for three hours at a time. She definitely guided me through the darkness as a compassionate talk therapist. When I had my divorce, I immediately went back to her. She is forever my spiritual mother. I cannot thank her enough.

• Evelyn Kuo was the first shaman in my life who helped crack my heart open. She was the first therapist who made me feel safe and held when she would put her hands on my heart. I cannot tell you the number of times I broke down on her treatment table or her Pilates equipment. The body keeps the score, and she was the first shaman who has reconstructed my physical body with Pilates and bodywork. I cannot thank her enough.

• The first day I met Master Sha, he saved my life. One crown chakra calligraphy blessing, and I found enough strength to go cold turkey on my addiction. Countless teachers at the Tao Academy empowered me and helped open my spiritual channels. Master Francisco, Master Rulin, I cannot thank Master Sha and everyone from the Tao Academy enough.

- Dr. Robert Chu gave me the confidence to start my healing career. He told me, "basics are already advanced, advanced is basics applied." Without his encouragement, I would not have had such confidence in my acupuncture practice. His most important contribution in my life is 大道至簡. He made everything easy to understand and learn. He taught me how to think and solve problems with clarity and penetration of acupuncture, but also with flexibility in implementation. The Tao is simple, and the Tao is infinite. I cannot thank Dr. Chu enough.

I can never thank John enough. For half my life, he has taken care of me and been my rock. He gave me everything he had. If I am anything, it's because of him. He was my biggest cheerleader, and his support made it possible for me to get my medical degree, study from all the great teachers and rediscover my light. For every positive karma that I generate in this world, a significant portion should credit John, for I am nothing without this man.

I can never thank my kids enough. On a daily level, I thank my kids for being a champion in going between two houses. On a bigger level, I thank them for their unconditional love, acceptance, and forgiveness for all the pain I have unconsciously put them through. On the highest level, I thank them for being the reason and motivation for change, courage, and strength. They are the fuel for my growth. Everything I do is because I want my kids to have a better future. I heal myself so that I don't perpetuate my wounds onto my kids. While everybody else will let me off the hook, my children are my anchor, my report card, the best feedback of what I would like to become. Because everything I want my children to have (e.g., the ability to receive love, forgive, self-soothe with compassion, be guided by their own light, be humble, live harmoniously with healthy boundaries, have abundance and be of service) is something I get to *embody* and *model* for my kids.

I can never thank my clients, readers, and students enough. I can't possibly accrue positive karma if they weren't willing to receive my help, healing, and wisdom. I am so nourished by my clients, readers, and students that I believe they accrue as much positive karma for receiving me as I do for serving them.

I can never thank my ancestors, my spiritual guides, divine, Tao, source enough for my abundance, guidance, and channel that helps me see the emptiness of my suffering. Without the love, support, and protection of my spiritual channels, it wouldn't have been safe enough for me to journey into the dark. Without the guidance of my spiritual channels, it would not have been possible for me to see the honest truth about me, whether it is the greatest darkness (e.g., murderer) or the greatest gifts that I am.

I can never thank my traumas enough. It is my traumas that provide the crisis for me to awaken.

I can never thank me enough. The relentless way you never stop learning, doing the shadow work, facing the truth, asking for help, and bouncing back stronger. I don't know anyone more dedicated, hardworking, or courageous than the way you show up to throw yourself in the fire and rise from the ashes.

My kids can never thank me enough, as I can never thank my parents enough. They can never comprehend the ways my love has nourished their growth. They can never comprehend all the gifts, from strengths to positive karma, that they have inherited from me.

John can never thank me enough as I can never thank him enough. He can never understand the love and support that has been pouring and is continuously available to him.

Nobody can ever thank me enough, just like I can never thank anyone enough. The source lives in them, and the source lives in me. How can anyone ever comprehend the extent of my magic? How can I ever comprehend the extent of their magic?

Thank you for recognizing that I can never thank others enough, and others can't ever thank me enough. We can finally give up seeking to be understood or appreciated. :)

If I am grateful for what I have, then I am already rich!

Me.

Now it's your turn! Post your letter on Instagram and tag @HonoringDarkness or post on the free Honoring Darkness Facebook group to share your story in community! #HonoringDarkness #GreatestEntitlement #ShadowWork

2.9

SHADOW OF SERVICE: MANIPULATING AND TAKING ADVANTAGE OF OTHERS

"I didn't mean to hurt you"—that's what I was told after I was raped. "There's no malicious intent"—that's what my co-parent would tell me after he took advantage of me, manipulated something in his favor, or hurt me *unconsciously*.

Up until this point, I have shared a lot about myself as a victim, as a rescuer. At the risk of everyone throwing rocks at me, I am going to tell you stories of me as a perpetrator—stories of how I took advantage of others and manipulated things to be in my favor. This is perhaps the most daring thing I have done. But it is so important for you to see my humanity and to see how taking ownership of my past has allowed me to step into my authentic power. I pray that instead of throwing rocks at me and judging me for my past, that my story will empower you to own your story.

The truth is, we are more connected than we can comprehend. In this world, everything is vibrations. Therefore, we are either generating win-win or lose-lose situations. When I offer a blessing, the healing has to go through me before it reaches another person. When I want to hurt someone, the curse goes through me before reaching another person. In other words, it always hurts me to seek revenge, and it always benefits me to uplift and empower others.

I want to own my inner perpetrator for *my* benefit because how I hurt others is also how I hurt myself. The part of me which manipulates, lies, and tears down others is also doing that to me—and because I was constantly manipulating, I had to guard against other people's manipulation constantly. In other words, how I didn't trust others was how I didn't trust myself. "Who only wants me for my wallet? Who only wants me for my body? Who only wants me because they have something to gain from me? Is he lying? Did he ever love me?" With this kind of defensive vibration, it was hard for me to form attachments to anyone and myself.

THE EXPERT SECRET KEEPER (AKA LIAR)

> When children learn through punishments and rewards, "they learn to lie and hide things that are punishable and only show the things that are worthy of being rewarded." -Parenting coach Sterna @sternasuissa.

By the time I was 17, I knew I was an expert secret keeper. I would lie for my friends to keep them safe from getting into trouble. When I was in college, I would let my friends copy my problem sets, knowing that I was enabling someone to commit plagiarism. During the 3.5 years affair, I wasn't only hiding it from John, but I was also lying and cheating myself. Even though I longed to have intimacy in the marriage, it was my dishonesty that prevented intimacy in the marriage.

MY GREED FOR POWER AND FOR MORE

When the 3.5 years affair ended, I was so relieved of my return to the light. I healed my body image and loved myself enough not to need another man's lust for my body to feed my ego. I was satisfied and grateful for John as a husband, but my thirst for more power led me to start another affair. At that point, Jay and I were friends who met at the yoga studio. I had medical intuition, and he had a vision. I offered an energy exchange—a transaction—so I would download his vision abilities, and he would download my medical intuition. And it worked.

Because Jay was sexually abused as a child, I felt safe around him. He entered my life during COVID, at a time when my marriage was put to the test, and there was a disappearing of support around me. John stopped taking walks, eating outside, seeing friends, or going on vacation. He was always on his screens, and I was isolated. Because of COVID, my shamanic healing with Evelyn, my yoga classes with Wahe Guru and Susan, my drum circle with Scott, and my friendship with Addison were all on hold. Jay filled a vacuum. He would walk with me and give me his presence. I enjoyed his company chanting mantras, practicing yoga, and meditating together.

Jay played the role of a rescuer but also a perpetrator. I was prey that he hunted. Or another way to look was that everything I needed was provided by the Tao. Since I was attached to my label as a victim, I naturally manifested a rescuer and a perpetrator. Two months into spending time with Jay, I didn't want to be in the dark like I did through the 3.5 years affair. I didn't want to hide like last time. So I asked John for the option of an open marriage. After listening to my stories, John was willing to forgive everything but gave me the option of a monogamous marriage or a divorce. We were in gridlock. I had a codependent relationship with both Jay and John. I couldn't give up either one because I felt like I couldn't live without either one. I was attached to both.

THE ULTIMATE MISTAKE LED TO THE ULTIMATE AWAKENING

As a victim, I felt tricked, betrayed, used, abandoned, rejected, disempowered, worthless, powerless, isolated, and resentful.

As a rescuer, I tried to fix myself. I tried to fix John. I tried to fix the relationship. I tried my best, and my best was still not good enough.

As a perpetrator, I pushed John away because I was scared because my ego cared too much about looking good, being right, and winning every fight.

But I needed to be a victim, a rescuer, and a perpetrator to have an awakening through my crisis. To realize the illusion of separation.

- When I was devastated to be rejected by John, it was me that I was devastated to be rejected by.

- When I was angry and resentful at John, it was me that I was angry and resentful at.

- When I didn't want to listen to John, it was me that I didn't want to listen to.

- When I accused John of being too scared for connection, it was me that was too scared for connection.

- When I accused John of being too egotistical and cared too much about getting his way, it was me that was too egotistical and cared too much about winning the argument during conflicts.

- *When I wanted John to regret letting me go, it was me that regretted letting John go and not being able to convince him that we could make it work. @#$%$.*

- When I blamed John for never apologizing and validating the pain he gave to me as a perpetrator, it was because I couldn't own how I had been a perpetrator to him.

- When I blamed John for taking me for granted and not thanking me enough, it was because I was taking him for granted and not thanking him enough.

- When I blamed John for not giving me another chance because I was already doing my best, it was because I couldn't forgive John and see that John was already doing his best.

It was me that created all of my illusions and sufferings. When John said, "I don't see a way forward" on the day that he decided on a divorce,

- It was me that pushed the cat into a corner and forced him to initiate the divorce and take the blame for breaking the family.

- It was me that was too proud to ask for another chance.

- It was me that was too scared and disconnected from my heart.

- It was me that didn't trust him or the strength of our friendship.

- It was me that was the perpetrator that broke the family and then escaped the responsibility as a victim.

@#$%^.

John said I only saw the good in people and that I didn't know how dark humans can be. It's actually John who only saw the good in me because I was so good at hiding my shadow. I was so good at looking good. I was so good at hiding all my junk from him and myself!!!!

@#$%^.

I was so attached to toxic positivity, always saying the right thing and doing the right thing, that I was completely lying and denying myself of my darkness. And I hurt everyone with my unconscious darkness—I hurt myself with my unconscious darkness.

"An unsafe person becomes angry and dismissive when you communicate your frustration, refuses to take responsibility for their behavior, projects their insecurities onto you, often lies as a way to avoid dealing with reality, does not forgive you for past mistakes and often brings them up in arguments."

-Nawal Musfafa

@thebraincoach

@#$%^! @#$%^! @#$%^.

This was me. I was an unsafe person, and that's why John had to leave me and set boundaries to block communications with me.

MANIPULATION IS PART OF THE TAO. IT IS NOT GOOD OR BAD

Remember the Yin Yang laws in the introduction? Within yin, there is yang, and within yang, there is yin. Yin and yang cannot separate. Yin needs yang to grow, and yang needs yin to grow. Yin and yang are constantly transforming into one another.

Manipulation is in everything. Shakti is our ability to manifest. Before we manifest and make anything happen, we first need to have a desire. Everyone has desires. Even to serve humanity is a desire. To bring love, peace, and harmony into our lives, to have good health, relationships and finances is a desire. Every thought and action, every communication comes with the desire.

There is no such thing as selfless service because that assumes that I give something to you, and I get nothing in return. Let's set up a math proof. Let "selfless service" be yang. Let "taking care of my needs" be yin. Since yin and yang cannot separate, since there is yin within yang, yang within yin, when I serve my kids, I am getting something in return. For example, I may get gratitude and positive karma, my ego may feel good about myself, I may feel proud, wanted, needed, and successful. When I take care of myself, I am serving my kids. If I don't take care of myself, I will be burned out, resentful, off-balance, angry, stressed, and tired. Therefore, when I serve you, I am serving me. When I serve me, I am serving you.

There is manipulation in everything. In every marketing email and website, it comes with the desire for you to take action. There is no spiritual teacher, healer, or nonprofit out there who can put out any communication without the vibration of desire for you to take action.

There can be a lot of love with manipulation. Manipulation isn't good or bad. Manipulation is the dark feminine force of manifesting our desire into reality. Taking something, conquering, dominating, mastering, accomplishing is the masculine force. Taking advantage of a situation can also be considered as making the best of what the Tao has given us.

Manipulation and taking advantage is what I am doing right now. I am taking advantage of my trauma, manipulating it into lessons, and transforming my pain into my strengths. Manipulation and taking advantage are part of the Tao. Everyone does it.

Everyone makes the best of the cards they are dealt, and it is just whether we are conscious or not. If we own our manifestation and become aware of it, we become powerful.

OWNING OUR DESIRE LEADS TO OUR SOUL PURPOSE

A lot of clients arrive, and they are in jobs or relationships that they don't love. They don't know what their soul purpose is, and their partner may not be the most aligned with their path. One time John told me if I remained a small-town local acupuncturist, we could stay together. He didn't want a wife that travels the world giving talks. I can be a victim and sit here and complain about how he is part of the patriarchy and doesn't want a powerful wife. Or, I can thank him for his clarity in knowing what makes him happy. I thank him for having the clarity that we are not compatible as he is not in alignment with my soul purpose of becoming an international teacher and a lifelong student. I can thank the universe for the perfection of everything that happened, for sending me a spiritual man who loves to walk in nature, practice yoga, chant mantras, travel, and is equal part science and spirituality. I can thank the universe for the perfection of sending me a man who can support me in my soul purpose, who loves to serve humanity as much as I do. I can thank the universe for delivering this man at the perfect timing so that he supported me through my crisis and my awakening. I can thank the universe for giving me a man that increased my service.

Service is about alignment. I am not for everyone. Not everyone is for me. If we let go of our attachments and surrender to God's plans, we can come into our greatest purpose of service.

Trust everyone's Yes and No. When someone requests our service, say yes with honor for the opportunity to serve. When someone doesn't want to be served by us, their rejection is serving me and helping redirect my energy.

Let go of people who aren't ready to love me yet, and who aren't ready to receive my service yet. What doesn't serve others doesn't serve me.

Trust our physical body, the body of our finances, and the body of our relationships. If our body is tired, rest. If our bank account is empty, allow ourselves to receive it. When we need a new lover / social media manager / client, allow the universe to send us help. Don't give what we don't have. Have you ever served others when you are tired? Have you ever given money to someone or a business that you don't have? Have you ever been too proud to ask for help? Some of us are overly attached to being the rescuer that we are doing a disservice to ourselves. What doesn't serve us doesn't serve others. Give up the struggle. Set boundaries with ourselves, so we don't do things that are not win-win.

REFRAME TAKERS AS A RECEIVER OF SERVICE AS OUR BUDDHA

By being the rescuer, John saw himself as the person who gave and me as one who took. After the divorce, he couldn't thank me for one thing that I have contributed to our 19 years of relationship. But the person who has less power, who asks and receives service, is the highest kind of service.

After Buddha achieved enlightenment, he continued to bring his begging bowl and knock door to door. On the surface, the person putting food in the Buddha's bowl is serving the Buddha. But actually, the Buddha is serving others by humbly giving others an opportunity to serve him.

- We serve by being the powerless victim asking for help.

- We serve by being the rescuer who gives help.

- We also serve by being the perpetrator who creates the opportunity for the person to know themselves and grow.

Because John did not validate my pain or apologize for hurting me, I got to experience the pain grow into hatred, overcome resentment and revenge, find closure, and practice forgiveness without his apology. Because of him as a perpetrator, I found my strength and courage.

Because John took me for granted and did not thank me for my 19 years of contribution, I got to experience worthlessness and self-doubt, overcome my source fracture, find my gifts and increase my service as a healer. Because of him as a perpetrator, I found my authenticity and my gifts.

Because John told the kids he didn't know if he could ever trust me again and blocked all communications with me except pickup / drop off, I got to experience my kids' rejection of me, overcome my fears in showing up, and find my fire and stand in my leadership power. Because of him as a perpetrator, I found my dedication and fierceness.

In Chapter 69 of Tao Te Ching, "There is no greater misfortune than underestimating your enemy.

Underestimating your enemy means thinking that he is evil. Thus you destroy your three treasures and become an enemy yourself."

Once I saw how I was able to make the best out of the pain that was given to me, I no longer fear being a perpetrator because how can I underestimate everyone else that they cannot bounce back like I did?

CHANGING FROM "HAVE TO" TO "GET TO"

I used to think of everything as a chore that I "have to" do. I have to wake up early and make my kids breakfast every day. Picking up and dropping off my kids is so stressful. I always have to sit in line and deal with all this traffic.

It took a divorce and only having my kids some of the time to really enjoy all the service I "get to" do. After I joined the "Alliance to Solve Parental Alienation", I realized how lucky I am to get my kids 50/50. So many people never see their parents/children after the divorce, but I get to cook breakfast for my kids. I get to sit in the line to pick up my kids.

Sometimes we have to lose someone or almost lose someone to really appreciate the opportunity to serve them.

Now, when my daughter tells me she just pooped but can't flush, I serve with joy. It's not selfless service, even though I don't ask anything in return. I receive so much from this transaction of cleaning the toilet bowl. I get to be a rescuer, I get so much joy, I get to show up for my daughter, I get to show my daughter how much I love her, and I appreciate this opportunity for connection so much.

GIFTS OF DARK FEMININE AND DARK MASCULINE

I have come to appreciate the gifts of the dark feminine in my great-grandmother, my grandmother, my mother, and myself.

The dark feminine is the mysteries of womanhood and magic, the chaos of creation and destruction, death and birth, transformation, rage, fierce compassion, seduction, and pure spiritual ecstasy. Sometimes the dark feminine shows up to control outcomes by complaining, nagging, manipulating, guilt-tripping, criticizing, shaming, and character-attacking. The rage and the fierceness of the dark feminine are a part of our ability to manifest and seduce. The dark feminine is potent magic. A woman gains access to her magic by owning her shame, self-doubt, trauma, repressed emotions, and desires basically by embodying this book! :)

A woman who has embodied her dark feminine allows a man to be in their dark masculine. "Dark masculine is the energy that knows how to be in charge, how to penetrate the space with presence and be assertive and dominant." Sofia Sundari. To elaborate on the dark masculine, Jonathan Jay Dubois, Ph.D., Shaman and archeologist, who holds a sacred brotherhood circle, says,

"There is an inner animal in each of us. The animal in me is a predator. He watches, he waits, and he pounces at the right moment. He sees something (or someone) juicy, and he wants to take a bite. If there is consent, he bites. The dark masculine in me fully embraces that animal. The dark masculine feels what is needed from his balls (or her ovaries) and acts. He does not hesitate. His power rises and acts decisively. The dark masculine sees when something is out of integrity and/or out of alignment and calls it out. He smells a rat, and his warning system goes off, and he protects himself and his loved ones from harm. When the dark masculine is defending you, he goes for the throat and lays waste to those who would hurt you. The dark masculine gaze can penetrate you to the bone and make you feel seen in a way that you have rarely experienced. The dark masculine can ravish you, devour you, and leave you breathless.

If out of balance or hidden from your sight, the dark masculine can be very dangerous. He can take what he wants without permission. He can hurt you without remorse. He can act in his own interest without thought for the welfare of others. His action, if unconscious or imbalanced, can cause pain. This is why the dark masculine is feared and has a bad reputation. However, when out of the shadows and received by the feminine, he can make your life exciting and juicy. He can make you feel cared for and protected. He can keep you warm on long, dark nights."

What protects us from the dark masculine and dark feminine energy of ourselves and others is by being authentic and unapologetically true to ourselves.

Our inner dark masculine and inner dark feminine protect us from others being critical, complaining, controlling, and dominating. It helps us see that whatever is in the other person is also in us.

Exercise: Sometimes, we don't serve. We stay small because we are afraid of the way others judge us. Let's practice manipulating (aka making the best) of the judgment others have given us as a gift to help us know ourselves better. When we turn others' judgment into clarity, we see that everything in the universe is useful and happens for us!

Suggested music: "I will always love you" by Whitney Houston

Hello. This is my ability to manipulate. I will take all the judgments others have said about me to help me find clarity and use them to benefit myself and know myself better.

I welcome and thank everyone for their judgment, helping me grow by bringing something into my awareness. No matter what others say, I choose to receive it with gratitude and use their feedback for my benefit.

When we know who we are, when someone gives us a negative judgment—we get affirmation that the "flaws" are actually features—which we absolutely love and stand proudly about.

These are some of the negative judgments I have heard (X) and how I have used them to gain clarity (☯) about who I am.

X - You are too messy and all over the place.
☯ - Why thank you, making the best out of the chaos and reading signs from the whole cosmos is precisely my gift.

X - You are too wounded and cry all the time.
☯ - Why thank you, my shadow work empowers me to help more people.

X - You are too far from seeing the truth.
☯ - Yes, indeed, there is always room to purify, but I am a total badass in facing my pain and am so grateful for all the transformation I have done so far to get closer to the truth.

X - You are too ignorant to the dark side.
☯ - I meet my darkness and know my monster well.

X - You are too greedy for spiritual power.
☯ - Yes, I love learning because I am nerdy. But I am very generous when it comes to empowerment. I immediately share any power I have with all my clients who are willing and ready to receive.

X - You are too grabbing for attention on social media.
☯ - Yes, I love connecting and spreading healing vibes.

X - You are too broken and lack integrity.
☯ - I am human, and I make mistakes. When I put myself back together, I shine and radiate light from the cracks. My self-forgiveness muscles are so strong!

X - You are to easygoing to create boundaries.
☮ - My primary healing element is water. Water flows, water is gentle, water is nourishing, but make no mistake, water is strong enough to shape the Grand Canyon. I may appear soft and flexible, but I am stronger than the rock

X - You are too unstable and changing too much, I don't know who you are.
☮ - Thank you for acknowledging how much healing and transformation I have done on myself.

X - You are too sensitive.
☮ - Yes, medical intuition is my gift. Compassion and spiritual communication are what I practice every day.

X - You are too self-centered to be considerate of my feelings, and I don't feel heard.
☮ - Thank you for acknowledging the self-love and self-compassion that I practice. I wish, with the most sincere heart, that every person can cultivate self-love and self-compassion so they can take ownership (instead of outsource) the responsibility of loving and hearing oneself to others. Self-mastery is what I practice

X - Your dreams are too ambitious.
☮ - Thank you for acknowledging my passion in my service to humanity.

X - You are too naive to believe in unconditional love.
☮ - I have been deeply humbled by many healing miracles—I am a complete believer in unconditional love (as a nerdy scientist who has done enough experiments). Love is the highest medicine.

Therefore I thank myself for being an excellent listener. I thank everyone for their judgments, helping me develop with clarity the perfection that I am. My heart radiates in the truth of who I am, which is love and connection. I am so loved by all of you. Thanks for helping me know more about myself.

Me.

Now it's your turn! Post your letter on Instagram and tag @HonoringDarkness or post on the free Honoring Darkness Facebook group to share your story in community! #HonoringDarkness #GreatestManipulation #ShadowWork

Watch the 12/1/21 episode of Unity and Oneness. Shift from "what can I do" (stuck in human do, do do) to "who do I get to BE". Kriya for liver colon stomach.

https://fb.watch/an3bEv55g3/

2.10

SHADOW OF ENLIGHTENMENT: SHAME, NOT KNOWING AND AVOIDING OUR DIVINITY, RESISTANT TO THE GOD/SOURCE/UNIVERSE PLAN

It was Easter Sunday 2021 that I had a resurrection, a rebirth. I had just gone to church with my brother and had a powerful service on forgiveness. Up until that point, the shame of everything that I had done was crushing me. I hated myself for all the people I have hurt. I couldn't stand myself as a perpetrator. I wanted to hurt myself. If my most trusted person gives up on me and leaves me, what is the point of living on this earth? If the people who are supposed to be my rock disappear on me, how can I live anymore? Life is too hard. Nobody sees me or appreciates me, I might as well give up. My daughters are on team daddy. I felt like I have lost their love forever. Nobody cares enough about me to show up for me. I might as well not exist.

I had been suicidal at ages 8, 13, and 24. Since becoming a mother at age 27, I have never dared to face the part of me that wants to give up and kill myself. This time is different. Since Jesus had come to me in 2018 and asked me to channel him, I had been calling on Him for healing miracles. I knew what I had to do. I prayed, "Dearest Jesus. I love you, honor you, and appreciate you. I cannot thank you enough. I deeply apologize for not knowing how much I am loved. Thank you for all the times I have channeled you to heal other clients. This time, I need your divine intervention. Please help me face my darkest shadow of giving up on myself and heal all the times in the present and past when I had been suicidal. I trust you completely as my guide, to love me, protect me and support me, as I journey to the darkest part of my psyche..." and off I descended to my darkness. I wish I could tell you more about what my journey looked like. It feels like a place of complete darkness, and I don't know how long I was there. When I reemerged, it was the greatest love and peace I had ever experienced.

The very next day, I had two clients who talked about being suicidal. I was truly amazed at how the universe works. The universe had not sent me any suicidal clients until I had overcome my own shadow. God loves me so much that God never gives me any situation that I am not ready for!!!

"Pain cannot be healed by hating yourself; it can only be healed by loving yourself." - Teal Swan

---

THE RESURRECTION AND REBIRTH

I am so blessed to have Dr. Raven Lee, author of "Unbinding the Soul: Awakening through Crisis and Compassion," as my spiritual teacher and psychotherapist. This book provided a simple model of healing, drawn from Jungian Psychology, Tibetan Buddhism, and neuroscience. That week, I called on Raven to hold space and offer her wisdom and compassion to help me awaken, develop, and celebrate my human spirit.

During this time,

• I found myself doubting and second-guessing every communication. I saw things from my view, and I also saw things from his view. I felt like I was going crazy, doubting every thought and every feeling. Everything was a question mark.

• I couldn't stand myself. I couldn't stand being in my body. Sometimes I just wanted to take a knife and cut myself open and take all the rotten pieces of me out. I couldn't find peace.

• Everything hurt so bad I wanted to stab myself in the head and cut my heart open to let the poison out.

• The more I felt like nobody was listening to me (John and my kids were blocking communications with me), the more I felt like nothing I did was ever right, the more I wanted to hate and attack myself.

• I kept invalidating myself, gaslighting myself, second guessing myself. Sometimes I felt so confused and so lost. The more isolated I felt from John and the kids, the more I felt like my opinions didn't matter. My needs are insignificant, my feelings are inconvenient, and everything I do just seems to make myself and others uncomfortable.

• I wanted to fix everything so badly that I took on too much of the blame.

Raven taught me that all our suffering is because we are attached to a story, a role, and an emotion. We can laugh when we realize the truth and the emptiness of our suffering. I was having a crisis because the old way *wasn't working*. This means there is an *opportunity*. In her Radiant Heart Meditation classes (which I highly recommend), she taught me the 3 A's:

• Appreciate the opportunity to release old trauma

- Accept

- Allowing the darkness. Not judge the darkness but look into the information.

Peace is a process. John is not the bad one. I am not the bad one. We are both just learning. Bring compassion to both.

LETTING THE MUD SETTLE

Raven shared that awakening is a dance: when we awaken, we *will have regrets*. Aaaagggghhhhhh!!!!! My single biggest regret was all the pain I have given my children while I was an unconscious parent. I carry so much shame and guilt about being a "bad mom". Raven said, "let go of the guilt! Yes, you have done things you wish you didn't do. *Compassion to self is understanding why you couldn't have been the kind of mother or partner you wanted to be.* Can you bring healing to the guilt? Can you be aware of the guilt? Can you breathe compassion into the guilt? Can you forgive yourself? Can you *hold dearly* the part of you that is guilty?"

"Making amends is not to make everyone happy. Apologize, but don't fix the past. Simply make a commitment that you will show up from now on. Don't parent with guilt. Guilt *clouds* you. Children can feel your energy and your guilt, and they will *take advantage* of your guilt. You don't even have to tell them what you did wrong. Just have to start showing up. Simply acknowledge how difficult it must be for their parents to go through a divorce, and your commitment to growing and making it safe for them."

"Keep bringing compassion to yourself. Keep praying, 'May my suffering be healed'. Don't judge. Every time you notice guilt in your awareness—breathe into the heart. Connect to the divine and allow yourself to melt in divine love. Allow yourself to ride the horse of guilt.

Hold yourself like a loving mother. Let the past be in the past. Just show up now."

KEEP SHOWING UP IN THE ARENA? EASIER SAID THAN DONE!

In 2018, I attended Tanishka's Inner Goddess Retreat[1], where I learned about boundaries for the first time. When I woke up from codependency with no boundaries, I swung all the way to the opposite extreme of independence with too many boundaries! <insert horrified emoji> I set boundaries with everyone, including my kids, to an extreme. When my kids were "too much" (aka when my unhealed wounds were triggered), I started giving myself "time outs". I started checking out, using boundaries as an excuse or shield. I would accuse everyone else of having negative vibes. I would put up boundaries and justify them as a righteous and protective measure out of self-love. During this time, my children felt abandoned and neglected. Their mother was not stable, and if they said the wrong thing, their mother would disappear into meditation.

Because my mom constantly judged and criticized me about every little thing (and I hadn't healed from it), my fear of repeating the same mistake made me go to the opposite spectrum of not speaking to my kids. I was so afraid that anything I said to them would hurt them. I let my fear of hurting my kids with my words prevent me from showing up as a parent. I was crippled by my rightcous perfectionist victim nerd. My kids felt like I didn't care about them. In reality, I was just swallowing everything I wanted to say and do. I was carrying oceans of love, not knowing how to express it. My extreme boundaries locked me in a tower of grief and isolation.

Guilt is dwelling on past performance. "I could have done better" or "I should have done better." But our fear of failure is also our fear of succeeding. Nobody succeeds without failure. Here's the thing. Nobody is born knowing how to bike. We all have to fall many times before we get it. Life is like this. It's not how many times we fall, how badly we are hurt, but how many times we pick ourselves up and try again.

Showing up to the arena is hard. The people who watch from the bleachers are going to judge us—they will either be jealous of our triumph or criticize our failure. Instead of fearing jealousy or criticism, find compassion for those who are too afraid to set foot in the arena to play their own game. They waste their energy watching others to *avoid their own greatness*.

Brené Brown tells us not to worry about the opinions of those who sit on the bleachers. Those who are in the arena will appreciate others for showing up. I can't agree more, but what if the judgment comes from the inside? What if the voice of our inner critic is so loud we become so afraid of making mistakes that we can't walk out to the arena? We can spend our lives worrying about being judged by others or ourselves, or we can gently remind ourselves, "what do I get to create now?"

THE REWARD OF SHOWING UP

I hope you make lemonade out of all the lemons, sugar, and water in your life. I hope you make the maximum use of this book as I have. After writing just the last chapter, by finally stepping out of the victim rescuer perpetrator roles, I repaired so much in my relationship with myself and my daughters. At breakfast this morning, I had woken up 40 minutes earlier just to make croissants for breakfast, at her request. I love being the rescuer, of course. But perhaps the croissants stayed in the oven for a touch too long —she didn't eat any. I observed my thoughts: "I woke up 40 minutes earlier just to make this for you, at your request, and now you don't want to eat it?"

In one sentence, I saw that I was a rescuer (I tried to fix her breakfast when she could have done it herself), a victim (she rejected my food and my love), and a perpetrator (I wanted to blame or shame her with my words). I cast a spell on myself by declaring, "I am not a victim, I am not a rescuer, and I am not a perpetrator. I release the judgment of my performance as a mom and as a cook. I release the attachment that my daughter needs to eat a big breakfast to go to school—she can buy something from the school cafeteria. I release the attachment to saving my daughter. I shall not rob her of her own lessons and spiritual journey." At that moment, my spell was so powerful it blew out a light bulb in the kitchen.

WHY DO WE HAVE SO MUCH SHAME? THE PATRIARCHY

Patriarchy gave us duality. Good and bad. We learn to be *proud* of our success and *ashamed* of our failures. We learn to favor the *light* and reject the *dark*. We *reward* good behavior and *punish* bad behavior. In other words, all of our dwelling, attachments, and resistance are *learned* and *trained* into our subconscious.

Who is the judge of good and bad?

Each one of us is born whole and perfect, but we all choose to disconnect from our original wholeness in order to survive.

So how do we let go of our shame triggers? Ultimately the key is to know that we are already divine and perfect. Don't let someone else tell us that we are wrong and feel shame. Trust our heart for the truth, which is love.

One of my spiritual teachers said, "Let's say there is a man who is color blind and sees sunsets as green. To him, green sunsets are the truth. His experience of the green sunset is his truth. We don't get to tell him that a sunset is not green. He should not feel any shame for experiencing sunsets as green. That is how God made him."

Why do we spend so much time arguing about what is right and wrong when *your truth is perfect,* and *my truth is also perfect?*

OPENING OUR HEART

For a long time, I wanted to keep punishing myself. I held on to the shame because I was afraid of hurting others or myself again. Here's the thing. *Every time I punish myself, I disempower myself, dim my own light, disconnect from my own and others' divinity.* How I didn't trust myself is how I didn't trust others. *By choosing to stay in shame, I kept making myself feel like a criminal, and I kept breaking my own heart.*

After the total heartbreak of the divorce, I was so afraid of letting love in. I had a boyfriend, but I didn't really fully let him in. I kept pushing him away. I would deny my heart's desires. I would not let him get too close. I would not trust that he really loves me. But how I don't fully give myself permission to receive his love is how I don't fully give myself permission to love myself.

As it turns out, my boyfriend was also doing the same. He was also not fully receiving me into his heart. Basically, I was vibrating "I'm scared to love," and he was also vibrating "I'm scared to love." Who is going to be brave and be the first one to trust the other? Who is going to be the first one to open their heart to love? I love the Prayer of St. Francis to help me be brave and be the first one to open my heart.

ENTERING THE ARENA

I'm taking a huge risk in telling my true story, but the reward is so worth it. Even if I lose all my clients, even if I lose respect as an acupuncturist, as a professor, even if I lose everything in the material world, even if I lose the respect of many, I gain so much intimacy with myself.

In being vulnerable, I am going to lose someone that is not in alignment with me, but I will also gain the fierce respect of my tribe. That I don't just "talk the talk," but I actually "live and breathe and embody" the shadow work of this book.

My authenticity is the most important treasure in my life. It is more important than any license or certificate. I know that whatever the blowback or negative consequences are, I can always reinvent myself. I trust that the universe will appreciate this book as much as I appreciate the healing that came with sharing my story.

GIFT OF SHAME

Shame shows up when there is room for improvements in our lives. Rather than allowing shame to cripple us, share it! Brené Brown says, "Vulnerability is the birthplace of connection and the path to the feeling of worthiness." Indeed, "Shame cannot survive empathy." Writing this book with my BFF healer, witch Ji has been the most healing experience. I don't think I could have birthed this book without the empathy from her, and I am just so lucky that she happens to be a Doctoral candidate in Psychology.

Brené Brown says, "Imperfections are not inadequacies; they are reminders that we are all in this together." I couldn't agree with her more. The same day I shared my darkest secrets, we created a trusting, safe space for Ji to share her shame too. Ji loves all of me, even the parts of me that I find hard to love. I am so grateful for my courage to share and for the connections with Ji that had been established on day one she came as my client as we bonded over our abortions.

Exercise: write a letter to ourselves about our deepest shame, then see how our deepest shame has motivated us into our greatest powers.

Suggested music: "Total Eclipse of the Heart" by Bonnie Tyler

---

Hello. This is the voice of my shame.

My greatest shame is the way I didn't show up for my children.

I am so sorry for not being more available. I am sorry I worked too much, which led to neglect as a parent. I am so sorry that I hid a lot. I am so sorry for the many times I denied you, didn't hear you, invalidated your feelings, and talked over you. I am asking for your compassion as to why, even though I love you so much, that I end up hiding. One word: shame.

Shame is the lowest vibration one can have. Shame is the feeling that I am bad. I am not lovable. Why is it that I am always cold? Because I basically don't like myself, I feel really deep shame.

Everyone experiences shame. The less we talk about it, the more we have it. Shame is a normal valid emotion, just like anger, fear, and sadness. All relationship conflicts start with shame. If we feel good about ourselves, if we feel good about who we are, why would we need to prove ourselves right? Why would we want to put someone down?

Connection is why we are here. Connection is what gives purpose and meaning to our lives.

Shame is the fear of connection. Shame is the fear of "if I really let you see the real me, I won't be worthy of connection, and I may not be able to love myself. I am afraid if we see how bad I am, you may abandon me, and I may stop loving me. Therefore I need to hide from the truth and not show up."

Because I was dwelling in my shame, I am sorry for the shame that I have given others. I'm sorry for any internal dissonance that I have caused. I am sorry for making you feel bad about yourself. I am sorry for making you doubt yourself. When I see you judging yourself harshly, when I see your self-hatred, self-sabotage, self-attacks, I know that I am responsible for putting those unkind thoughts you have towards yourself. I am sorry for the poison I had put into you as a parent.

The good news is that spiritual practice helps us accept who we are and have a right to be in the world. Shame helps us identify the gaps in self-love.

Can we let go of expectations and judgments together? Can we embrace the perfection of us together? Can we empower and uplift each other? Can you please show me the parts of you that are difficult to love? Will you let me love every ounce of your being, including those that you were taught to hate or be ashamed of?

Greatest love

Me

Now it's your turn! Post your letter on Instagram and tag @HonoringDarkness or post on the free Honoring Darkness Facebook group to share your story in community! #HonoringDarkness #GreatestShame #ShadowWork

Ready to live your life to the fullest? Watch the 9/29 Live with Passion. Do what we are born to do, what makes our heart sing, what makes us feel in love. Remove our secret commitments that keep us from our passion and purpose.

https://fb.watch/an3CrxeFHO/

REDEMPTION: MY PARENTS SHOWING UP

How we show up for others in relationships is how others show up for us. Remember in Chapter 2.2 how my parents were unable to show up for me and in Chapter 2.3 how I was unable to show up for my kids? Well, the past is in the past! My children are so blessed to have a fierce tiger for a mother, and I am so blessed to have a fierce tiger for a mother too!

During COVID, when Hong Kong was in a strict lockdown, everyone who visited the United States had to be quarantined in a room for 21 days. They were not allowed to open any window or leave the room. It was essentially a prison with no fresh air. What did my mother do?

To the disbelief of all her friends, she came to support me, so I would not have to spend my first Christmas post-divorce alone and sad. The very day that she was leaving Hong Kong, the government announced that due to the contagious nature of omicron, residents returning to Hong Kong were required to stay in a detainment center for seven days. This place was basically a prison cell. There were days with electricity blackouts, no cell phone service, sporadic water, and food distribution, no towels, no delivery, and no take-out. Do you know what my mother did? She got on the plane. Even if it turned out to be a one-way ticket, she came (the Hong Kong government closed the borders and did not allow any planes from the US to land in Hong Kong). Even if she caught COVID during her stay, she came. She loved me so fiercely that she was going to visit me no matter what price she had to pay. None of her friends can understand her "craziness", but as her daughter, I cannot be more proud and grateful to receive her highest act of love.

Nothing awakens the courage and strength in a woman than when her babies are in pain. Sharing our pain asks the people who love us to step up. If I hadn't been open about my pain and cried on the phone so much, my mom wouldn't have become the badass that she is today.

"Your child is here to show you something about you. Look in the mirror of their eyes and discover your truth."

-Dr. Shefali Tsabary

Conscious parent and psychologist @doctorShefali

---

1. www.themoonwoman.com

PART III

JI'S JOURNEY INTO HER SHADOWS

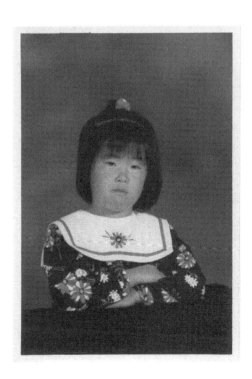

3.1

SHADOW OF LOVE: REJECTION, ISOLATION, LONELINESS AND GRIEF

THE CREATION OF A DEEP WOUND

One of my deepest wounds is abandonment and the fear of being left behind because I am either never good enough or "too much." This wound was created in the summer of 2003. I was ten years old and had just finished the 5th grade. My mom and dad thought it would be nice for my sister and me to go to Korea to visit our aunts, grandparents, and the rest of my family during the summer. My sister, Lucia 언니, and I had special treatment on the plane because we were both minors and traveling without our parents. I remember being excited about going to Korea and being able to spend all this time with my sister. My sister is four years older than me. It's just the two of us, and because of our age difference, we didn't always go to school together. My sister and I have always been close, and I was so happy to be able to spend every day together, without school or extracurriculars to keep us apart. The summer in Korea was going to be a sister bonding experience, and it started out so fun, even though it was hot and humid.

We went to Lotte World, we ate delicious food, and we got to spend time with both of our aunts traveling between Seoul and Daegu.

In the middle of our trip, our mom told us she would be suddenly coming to Korea. I didn't think too much about it. I was ten and figured she missed us too much. When she arrived, the look on her face showed me that something was wrong. My first thought was: did Dad die? Thank God the answer was no. But what followed would create a massive wound.

My mother told my sister and me that she was divorcing our dad. She told us that she's been having an affair for two years with a man who would soon become our "stepdad." Our mom told us that while we have been in Korea, she had been slowly packing our things. She informed us that instead of flying home to Salinas after our trip, we would be flying to Texas, where we would be living from now on. I sat in shock as our "soon-to-be stepdad" came into the room, and his presence was like a slap to my face. My shock transformed into deep pain, and I wept. I wept into my mom's arms and shoulder, soaking her clothes in my tears and snot. I was so deeply hurt that I would bite my mom's shoulder to keep myself from wailing. I would eventually sob myself to sleep.

The next few days and weeks were a blur. Even now, I only remember snippets or freeze frames of certain moments. I remember walking in the streets of Seoul with my mom, sister, and this bastard of a man and thinking how weird it felt to be playing a fake family. All I could think about was my dad. How was he doing? What would he tell us right now if he could talk to us? Was he okay?

When we left Korea and arrived in Houston, Texas, it was so hot and humid, the thickest heat of summer. We were staying in an acquaintance's friend's house as guests. I wondered how much the family we were staying with knew about our story. The only thing I remember about staying in Houston was us touring the different schools my sister and I were going to attend in the Fall and watching reruns of The Fresh Prince of Bel-Air. I thank God for Will Smith; he made that summer bearable and brought me joy and laughter during a time of intense pain. The show was a reprieve from the reality of my broken family. Here was Will, loved by his extended family and accepted into a close-knit family that was whole and together. I remember admiring Uncle Phil and Aunt Vivian's relationship, a true partnership where both respected and adored the other.

What felt like months after our arrival in Houston, my mom told my sister and me that we were going back to Salinas to see our dad, say goodbye, and return before school started. The night before our departure, my sister pulled me aside and told me to pack more things as we were not going to return. I understood what she meant, and I didn't ask any more questions. Because for me, I didn't care whether I lived with my mom or dad. All I wanted was to follow my sister wherever she went. If she wanted to live in Salinas with our dad, Salinas it was. I didn't choose to live with my mom or my dad.

I chose my sister. Everything felt chaotic and unstable, but my sister and our love for each other was the only choice I needed to make. To this day, my sister will *always* be my first choice.

THE WOUND GETS BIGGER

We arrived in Salinas, and finally, we were back home. Except home felt completely different than the last time we were here. *Before* we left for Korea. *Before* our family was broken. *Before* my heart was shattered. The house even looked different. Our rooms were bare, some furniture was gone, and the house was a mess. Not only did the house feel empty, but the life behind my dad's eyes was empty. His light was gone.

When my wound was created in Korea, my light diminished and was already leaking out of me slowly. By the time we arrived in Salinas, my light was so dim I felt like a ghost or an empty shell of what I once was. When I looked into my father's eyes, my light also completely vanished. Poof, it was gone at ten years old. I could clearly see his marred heart on his emotionally scarred face. My dad was in so much pain. As I clearly saw my dad's inner child in panic and confusion, my childhood completely stopped, and I became an adult. My inner child shut down. I felt this intense responsibility to save my dad from his anger, pain, and grief.

The few days leading up to the scheduled flight back to Texas, I called my mom and told her my sister and I would not be coming back. I was sobbing and in excruciating pain as I asked my mom to mail our stuff to us. The pain in my mom's voice is the type of grief only a mother separated from her child could feel. My heart broke while I broke my mom's heart. She never thought about the possibility of us living with our dad instead of her. The way my mom's grief hurt her was the way my grief hurt me too. I never wanted to hurt my mom like that again.

I was parentified at ten years old and became the emotional parents to both my mom and dad. I felt the need to save my mom from her grief and save my dad from his pain. My dad would cry every night, and his sobbing broke my heart. I could see how traumatized he was from when my mom left him and because he thought he was losing my sister and me too. I would do everything I could to protect my parents from feeling any more pain, even if it meant that I would pay a high price too. Being so young, I didn't know at the time what the cost would be until later into adulthood.

My dad was so hurt and afraid of losing us again that we would all sleep in the big primary bedroom for the first few months of living with him. There was the big bed that my mom and dad used to share and a foldout mattress on the floor. My sister and I would sleep on the bed while my dad slept on the floor. These months were the most fragile time for all three of us. We were trying to figure out what our "new normal" would be.

In the first year of living with my dad without my mom, I stopped all extracurriculars and spent all my energy and time on my parents. I would make sure to be home right after school at the same time every day to talk on the phone with my mom. It was important to pick up the phone at our scheduled time because it was when my dad was away at work. During these daily phone calls, and for an entire year, I begged my mom to come back.

In my ten year old mind, any decision could be reversed. I fully believed that my mom could come back, my dad would forgive her, and we could all be together again. Every chance I had to make a wish, whether it be a birthday candle or a car drive in a tunnel, I would wish and pray with desperation that my mom would come back.

After a year of begging my mom, I finally stopped asking her to come back. I knew it was breaking her heart every time she had to tell me that she couldn't. Even though I stopped asking her, I didn't stop wishing. Daily prayers didn't work. Searching for shooting stars didn't bring her back. I felt betrayed by God and internalized that I must be bad if my prayer went unanswered. I would learn to hate myself fiercely.

I felt so much grief. I felt like I had lost my mom forever. I saw how heartbroken she was that my sister and I weren't living with her. I saw how she never planned for us not to be with her, and I hated myself for being the reason for her pain. I also hated everything about me because I believed I must not be worthy enough for my mom to come back for.

LOVE IS ALWAYS THERE

Even though my central wound of abandonment has been one of my biggest areas of healing, part of my healing has been to look for the love that was present. The shadow of love is denying the love you have already around you. Being a young child, it made sense that I was deeply hurt over my parents' broken relationship. It was as if love no longer existed. But I was completely wrong. Love was always there. I was blind to seeing how much love my sister and I had for each other.

My sister, Lucia, is the most important person in my life. Words cannot fully capture or comprehend how much she means to me, and no amount of "I love yous" can show her how much unconditional love I have for her. She is my favorite person, and I am grateful to be blessed to have a sister like her in my life. Consider yourself rich and blessed if you have at least one sibling to fiercely love and have that love reciprocated back tenfold.

The love we share is an unbreakable bond that transcends lifetimes. My sister has been my biggest inspiration. She has an unbreakable focus and concentration for righting all wrongs that amazes me to this day. I am who I am because of our relationship and the love we share. We are different but also so much the same. My inability to see the love that was already strong in our separated family was the biggest obstacle I had to overcome. I was stuck in my loneliness that I was isolating myself. I was too protective over my heart, afraid of loving others, and even more scared of *being* loved. My sister was the only one I wasn't afraid to love. Her love for me taught me to melt my heart open and let Love, with a capital L, truly in.

"As a spiritual seeker, I understand that this journey requires you to not only embrace all that is whole and good in your life but also to continually examine the long-buried wounds hidden beneath your carefully crafted surface. This is what I mean when I say, 'Turn your wounds into wisdom'."

— Oprah Winfrey

3.2

SHADOW OF FORGIVENESS: ANGER, HOLDING GRUDGES, HATE, AND RESENTMENT

PAIN TO RAGE

From my biggest hurt as a ten year old, I would grow angry, and that fury would just simmer and boil over in endless cycles. To protect myself from being ever hurt again, I put walls up. I would refuse to ever be hurt again. I never wanted to feel the pain I went through, and for years, anger would be my armor. It would take me almost two decades to finally let my armor down. Letting go of my anger was one of the hardest things I have ever done, and this is a big part of my story.

MY RELATIONSHIP WITH RAGE

I *hated* when people would tell me about forgiveness. Whenever I heard this word, a little flame of rage would ignite in the back of my throat. This was because forgiveness, in my mind, was absolving the accountability of others who have harmed me. I would feed all my grudges with their favorite snacks: pain, rage, and destruction. If I didn't feed my grudges consistently, I had a fear that I would be condoning the harm and hurt that others have inflicted on me.

I didn't know who I was without my anger. I felt like I only existed for my rage and that I was only alive to constantly feed it. My anger was my drive, my fuel, and my *every* motivation. It was the only emotion I was in touch with and was my "go-to" feeling and reaction.

I was in a love/hate relationship with rage.

Rage made me feel powerful and untouchable. It gave me the strongest weapons—to dole out third-degree burns or leave the smallest stings. With anger, I had the potent force not just to hurt but annihilate. Seeing the destruction I created was *exhilarating*.

However, my rage also scared me. I was afraid of what my anger could do and how quickly I could tap into the limitless potential to obliterate. I hated how instantly I hurt people I love and the feelings of guilt and shame that quickly came right after I raged.

A LITTLE BIT OF CONTEXT

I grew up in Salinas, California. I was born in Oceanside, but my family moved to Salinas when I was only two or three years old. The part of Salinas I grew up in was a community full of mostly people of color. There were a lot of undocumented folks, and I am grateful that I was born in the U.S. and that my mom, dad, and sister had green cards. Although I grew up with people of color all around me, there were not many Asian people in Salinas. Then with the small population of Asian people, there was even a smaller amount of Korean people.

The beauty of Korean people is that you can find us *anywhere*. My sister has visited India and met Korean people, even eating Korean food. She met Korean people in Uganda. We are everywhere.

In Salinas, there was a small Korean church that my family attended, and that was our community. My sister and I would grow up having multiple parental figures and brothers. In my church, everyone knew how much I loved presents and toys. I would gladly accept gifts, even from Korean elders at the church that I was not very fond of. But I remember there was a man, I'll call him Church Dude, who gave me presents and I never wanted to accept them. I would refuse his gifts. My mom would tell me it's rude to refuse gifts, so I would reluctantly accept them but would never play with any of the toys Church Dude got me. At the young age of five or six, I knew in my deep soul that I did not like this person. My intuition told me to *never* let my guard down around this man.

Remember in the previous chapter, when I talk about the affair my mom had for two years with the man she would eventually leave my dad for? It was with Church Dude. Church Dude was someone I knew most of my life and never trusted. My family and his family all attended that same small town Korean church in Salinas, and we were all in the same community.

Church Dude became Mom's Dude, and I hated him with every cell in my body. Not only did he betray my dad's trust, but he tried to become our dad. NO. NO. NO. Since I was ten years old, I was raging, and it would emanate 24/7. My fury would radiate in every vibration and energy I gave out because it was my survival mechanism. My intuition knew that intense rage would keep me protected from him.

HOW MY STEADY RAGE TURNED INTO AN UNCONTROLLABLE WILDFIRE

I had a habit of falling asleep in the living room, and one morning when I was 18 years old, I woke up to what felt like a kiss on my lips. As I fluttered my eyes open, I saw Mom's Dude hovering over me, trying to kiss me again. I fought him off and screamed NO!!!! I quickly realized that my mom and sister weren't home for some reason. I panicked, but because my anger was so instant and searing, he was already out the door on his way to work. The ignited rage in me turned into a smoldering, whipping wildfire.

Because my rage was like shrapnel in my waking hours and quietest when I was sleeping, Mom's Dude's only opportunity to violate me was when I was asleep, and nobody else was home. This overwhelming realization washed over me. It also confirmed what I had known all this time—I am unsafe around him. For years, I felt watched in my own home, and home never felt safe. It validated all the times I felt paranoid about getting fully dressed after every shower I took, locking the bathroom door when he was home, and the frequent nightmares I would have of him attacking me.

But the worst wasn't over.

I told my sister, and she urged me to tell my mom. After telling my mother, she denied my experience. Now gasoline was being poured on my wildfire rage. She told me that he must've thought I was peaceful looking in my sleep and wanted to show me sweet affection—that it was probably harmless.

I pushed my experience deep down. I wouldn't tell another soul until years later. Eventually, I would start to gaslight myself and tell myself I may have misinterpreted what happened. Was I *truly* violated if he didn't try anything more with me after kissing me? Am I confused? Could I be trusted?

For years, I told myself that maybe it wasn't a violation because he didn't try anything sexual with me. I questioned if him kissing me was sexual. Was it or was it not? I would start not to trust myself. I would gaslight myself, and I didn't even call it a violation until years later.

However, my anger grew and grew. I was full-on raging and thrashing. I hated Mom's Dude with every bone, muscle, and fiber in my being.

Eventually, it would take me years to see that I hated my mother more than I hated Mom's Dude. Even though he hurt and violated me, the biggest burn was my mother's reaction. I would only be able to address the anger I had for my mom a few years later when I started therapy.

WHEN I MET THE MURDERER IN ME

I remember a time that I was so angry I was close to murdering. Mom's Dude and I got into a fight and a power struggle. He was trying to parent me when it had been established that he could *never* parent me. This also happened not long after he violated me. I grew into such an intense rage that all I could see was red, and all I could feel was extreme heat all over my body. My face and ears were boiling with fury. All I could think about was the gun I knew he kept in the house. All I could fixate on was how to load the bullets and whether I should aim for his stomach, head, or penis. In that moment, I understood in my entire being how second-degree murder happens. The heat rising in me felt like I *must* hurt him in the heat of *this* moment. I desperately wanted to cause him the pain he caused me and show him: DON'T YOU DARE MESS WITH ME.

What happened next was truly a Source/God/Soul/Divine/The One/Spirit intervention. I screamed into my pillow so hard to muffle the sound of my pain, and as I sobbed, the heat in my face, ears, hands, and body dissipated. I felt what was the quietest of heart whispers: "You can't do what is meant for you from jail." While laying down with tears streaming into my ears, I fell asleep. I thank my Spiritual Guides every day for their intervention. I feel like The One winked at me and gave me the miracle of slumber.

Even though I woke up the next day no longer wanting to murder, I awakened to the murderer in me. My rage wasn't fully gone because I was still living in a sea of fury, with my anger just ebbing and flowing and always present. Meeting the murderer in me scared me. The potential of my anger led to me further distrusting myself.

THE ROOTS OF MY ANGER

In my first few years of therapy with my current therapist (who I will refer to as M), I started looking under the rage. At this time, I started to see that I've been denying my anger towards my mom and directing all my rage at Mom's Dude. He wasn't undeserving of my rage, but it was *her* I was really mad at. I couldn't see the depth of my rage because I *needed* my mom. I loved her. I didn't *want* to hate her. I pushed every urge to hate her so deep down that it would leak out in other ways. I turned passive-aggressive towards her. I resented her. Eventually, it got so bad that I would say the most hurtful things to her.

The opposite of love is not hate but indifference. I didn't really care about Mom's Dude. He was just the easy scapegoat for all my rage. However, I cared about my mom. Because I loved my mom so much, I also really hated her. I hated her for not believing me when I told her about him violating me. I hated her for turning my life upside down when she decided to divorce our dad and move us to Texas. I hated her for never choosing me. I hated her for always choosing Mom's Dude over me. I hated her for not seeing how much she was hurting me.

I would beg my mom to leave Mom's Dude. I could see how she felt trapped in this relationship but also, I wanted her to *choose* me. By spending years begging my mom to leave Mom's Dude, I would be retraumatized with the pain of when I begged her to come back to Salinas when I was ten years old. Every time she told me she couldn't, I would be reminded of my pain of being told no back then. I would eventually put her in an impossible ultimatum: she would either have to choose me or Mom's Dude. She chose neither, and I hated her for it. Since I was ten years old, the hate I felt for myself has always been in me, and that hate would also be the way I hated my mom. I would yell at her, "You shouldn't have become a parent if you weren't ready to show up for me." I would scream, "You don't love me because you will always choose him." We learn to hate others by the way we learn to hate ourselves, and this is exactly what happened between my mom and me.

My hate would grow, and eventually, when I was 24, I told her that I didn't want a relationship with her and that I wanted nothing to do with her. I decided that if she wasn't going to choose me, I would make the choice for her. That night, she sobbed all night, and I didn't feel an ounce of guilt or remorse. Shortly after, I decided to finally move out. I gave her no warning and packed my things, and left. I left her the way she left my dad in Salinas. She didn't know where I lived for almost an entire year. I completely shut her out. I kept my word that she would have nothing to do with me.

BELOW THE RAGE

Cutting my mom out was what I needed at the time. I needed strict boundaries with her so I could release myself from how enmeshed I was with her. I also needed the time to be present with my rage. What I learned was that below the rage was my deep pain. I was so deeply hurt that I was lashing out.

I took this time to validate and honor my pain. I would finally let myself cry the tears I didn't let myself cry all those years. I was mourning the loss of my childhood and how it was the way I survived. I saw that my inner child was so heartbroken and fragile. I could see that my anger was my coping mechanism and how much I depended on the rage to protect me.

I started to see the truth that although I felt trapped by my anger, it protected me in many ways. Rage served me in shielding me from Mom's Dude trying to violate me in other ways. Anger prevented me from being taken advantage of by others. Anger protected me from my deepest pains. It gave me fuel to wake up in the morning rather than getting stuck in despair.

Taking the time to shed the tears I was holding inside was heartbreaking. I felt completely raw and highly sensitive. By feeling the deep pain I buried so long ago, I was releasing myself from being bound to my suffering. Anger was no longer my "go-to" emotion. I was letting other feelings in too. I was still in touch with anger, but I was also able to connect with my feelings of sadness, shame, guilt, joy, remorse, love, and fear instead of ignoring them.

CHOOSING FREEDOM

By letting emotions in other than rage, I was able to ease some of my tight grasp I had on my grudges. I was holding on to my grudges as if I could only let them go whenever my mom came around and took responsibility. I realized that I couldn't wait for my mom to be sorry in order for my healing to begin. I learned that by constantly waiting, I was keeping myself prisoner to my suffering. I was getting in the way of me when truly, I just wanted to be free.

Then, it clicked. I *finally* understood the true meaning of forgiveness.

Forgiveness is freedom. It is releasing the need to seek revenge, letting go of resentment, and unclenching the tight fist committed to vengeance. Freedom is not condoning or excusing the harm. It also does not mean reconciliation. Importantly, forgiveness does not mean forgetting.

When I understood that the pursuit of freedom is through forgiveness, was when I finally got it. Holding on to my anger was not holding my mother or Mom's Dude accountable, but it was just rotting me. My rage was not just incinerating others but was burning my heart and body to a crisp from the insides. I started to see that my rage won't wake my mother up to take accountability. I no longer wanted to live just to be the prop that constantly holds a mirror to my mom's face that asks: Do you see now? Have you seen what you have done?

So I forgave her—not for her, but for *me*. I let go of my need for my mom to be accountable and take responsibility for her actions. I let go of making it my life's mission to hold up the mirror to her face. I instead turned the mirror around to myself and started asking myself: What was I not looking at? Can I see what I have done? I released my need to hear, "I'm sorry." I was choosing to be free.

Letting go is a lifelong process, and it is not easy. It took me a long time to understand forgiveness, but I would rather be late to it than to never arrive. My road to freedom has been me taking one step at a time while letting go and shedding another layer with each step forward. Every single morning, I choose freedom.

"Forgiveness is giving up the hope that the past could be any different. It's accepting the past for what it was and using this moment and this time to help yourself move forward."

— Oprah Winfrey

3.3

SHADOW OF COMPASSION: NOT LISTENING, UNDERSTANDING, AND ACCEPTING OF SELF AND OTHERS

STILL KEEPING A DISTANCE

Even though I forgave my mom, I didn't know if I wanted a relationship with her. Remember, forgiveness does not mean reconciliation. Almost a year into cutting her out, I continued to be rigid with my boundaries with her. But deep down, I *missed* her. I missed having a mom. I missed the unconditional love that only a parent can provide. I was attached to having strong boundaries, so I didn't listen to myself missing her. I continued to keep my distance because I didn't trust myself or my voice fully.

However, I kept coming back to something my mom said to me. One of the last things my mom told me before I shut her out was that she would love me forever, no matter what. I could hate her and not want her in my life, but her love for me would never waver. And that if her being out of my life is the best thing for me, that she would stay out of my way. When she first told me this, I dismissed it as a way to manipulate my feelings. Yet, as I yearned for my mom's love and embrace, I saw how loving that is: to be in perpetual grief knowing that you are respecting your daughter's wishes.

I was missing her, but I wasn't reaching out to her. Because of my central wound of being abandoned, I didn't trust her love for me. But most of all, I didn't trust myself around her. What if I get angry again? What if I get hurt again? What if I lost all the work I did with creating boundaries and became enmeshed with her again? I was afraid of reaching out. I was frozen, and I kept pushing down my feelings of wanting to see her. Missing my mom led to deeper reflection.

BLOSSOMING COMPASSION

Just like a wildfire of rage can happen from the tiniest flame, the smallest spark of compassion ignited in my heart and blossomed. I vividly saw that she has been in survival mode since birth. I saw the lineage of ancestral and intergenerational trauma flowing through me from my mother, her mother, my grandmother's mother, and so on. I understood that my mom *couldn't* validate my trauma not because she didn't *want* to but because her survival depended on being blind to the truth. With clarity, I saw that her wounds were fully open and raw.

My mom is also a child of divorce, during a time in Korea where divorce was uncommon. She has had her share of trauma in her childhood. Her childhood wounds were not healed, and I could see that her survival mechanism was to be small and non-threatening to anyone around her. She learned to self-abandon, and I could see how hurt she was. The way we show up for others is the way we show up for ourselves, and so how could she show up for me? I saw how all the ways I hated my mom were the same ways I hated me: invalidating others' experiences and invalidating my experiences, not listening to myself and others, and rejecting Source in others leading to rejecting Source within me.

LETTING COMPASSION FULLY IN

I started to let the compassion I had for my mom fully in. I started seeing her as a different soul and spiritual being rather than my mom. I saw her humanity and how she was trying her best. I realized that my mom was not consciously rejecting me but that she couldn't see past her own pain. Instead of punishing her humanness, what if I loved all of her? The way I have compassion for others is the way I have compassion for myself. What if I started at home?

By having compassion, I could let my mom fully into my heart and learn to accept her love as unconditional and true. Before, I couldn't see how much loving space she was holding for me. By letting go of my distrust, I was able to also let go of my need to be defensive with her. I could lay my armor down. I could hang up all my weapons and go to her slowly with my arms open wide. I no longer needed to be hypervigilant in seeking any signs of potential harm or attacks. The truth is that *I was never at war with her*. She was stuck in conflict with herself, and the same was true for me. I had to finally bury the skeleton of my attachment to the narrative I held about how my mom abandoned me and that I will always be the young forgotten child.

I realized that my continuing to push her out was not only hurting her, but I was also depriving myself of love. I could heal and love her with compassion without expectations. This was compassion *with* wisdom. I learned that I could have a relationship with my mom without the need for her to take accountability. That even if she can't be sorry for her actions, I would still love her.

During the time we weren't speaking, and I was healing in my own way, my mom was also doing her own healing. She told me that the moment I chose myself, even though it hurt her that I didn't want a relationship with her, she was very proud of the fact that I was strong and chose myself. My mom started to do her own shadow work and face her own wounds. She saw how far she got away from herself by continuing to self-abandon. She started connecting to her own self. My mom started to see that the way she wasn't listening to my anger was the way she was rejecting looking at her wounds. By stepping fully into herself and seeing how the ways she didn't listen to me were the ways she didn't listen to herself—she blossomed.

In this time, she also ended up leaving Mom's Dude. My mom left him not just for my sister and me but for herself. She decided that even if her daughters didn't want a relationship with her, she couldn't continue in the relationship with Mom's Dude. She *also* chose her freedom.

MENDING WITH MY MOM

After the time of silence, I asked my mom if we could go on mother-daughter dates. I initiated once a month dinners and every other week coffee hangs. She was so excited that I broke the silence, and she was, of course, happy to do so. It was on these dates that we got to share our healing stories and the shadow work we have been doing on our own. The dates were my way of learning how to trust myself around her and also trust her. It was this valuable time that we built a strong foundation of trust and even more compassion. These moments were where we each got to stitch our own wounds back up, mend our relationship with each other, braid our stories together, and interweave our healing. I would eventually tell her where I lived. I would eventually invite her into my apartment. I invited her into my home, my heart, and my embrace.

I was 25 years old when I asked her to go on these dates. I highlight my age because the timeline of my hurt, anger, lashing out, revenge, compassion, and forgiveness has been over a long period of time. It wasn't just a one-year or two-year process. It was over years of processing, and there is no timeline for healing. Trusting the process and perfect Divine timing is what led me back to my mother's arms.

The funny irony is that when you let go of your desperate need is when it decides to show up. As I stood in the huge cemetery of all my deaths and grieved while in the process of welcoming the joy of my rebirths, what I no longer needed showed up like a blessing at my feet. On our first date, my mom took accountability. She deeply apologized from her heart for the hurt she caused me. Because my heart was already open to her, I could fully accept and embrace her apology. The most beautiful part is that I already forgave her before she apologized. Forgiveness is freedom, and I was *already* free.

I am so deeply grateful that our relationship has truly blossomed with every step we take on our own growth journeys. The gift of our conflicts is that we have inspired one another to reconnect with ourselves *through* the experience of reconnecting with each other.

My mom has thanked me numerous times for never giving up, even when I temporarily shut her out. And I thank her always for never wavering in her love for me and for continuously holding space for me. The truth is that she never abandoned me. She just needed to find herself to show up for herself and me. I learned how to be a generous receiver by basking in the warmth of my mom's infinite love.

LEARNING HOW TO BE A GENEROUS RECEIVER

My relationship with my mom has taught me how to be a generous receiver. My past trauma with her and my dad trained me to never fully receive love because it always came with a caveat. My past prevented me from asking for help even when I needed it. However, in the past few years of our relationship blooming and growing, my mother has shown me to trust and let love and aid fully in.

This past year in 2021, while I was going through a tough time with a close friend of mine, my mom fully showed up. It was tremendous healing for the both of us. I always struggled with asking for help, especially from my mom and dad. However, because I was in so much pain and hurt, my mom took care of me in ways that she couldn't take care of me in the past. I finally surrendered and asked for her help.

I stayed at her home for almost an entire month. My mom cooked for me and nurtured me as I cried in pain. She fed me with the most comforting Korean meals, and each bite was flavored with her healing elixir of love and compassion. It was healing for me to be able to receive the care that I didn't get at ten years old. It was healing for her to be able to give the love and care that she couldn't give after the divorce. We got to have a corrective emotional experience with each other.

Dr. Irvin D. Yalom talks about the corrective emotional experience in his book *The Gift of Therapy*[1] in relation to how the therapeutic relationship between therapist and client can be a corrective emotional experience in itself. However, I got to have that experience with my mom, the same person I had the traumatic experience with. It is so rare to have a corrective emotional experience with the person with who you had the original hurtful experience with, and to have that in this lifetime is one of the biggest blessings. This has taught me the lesson of surrendering to being a generous receiver as I ran into my mother's arms.

---

1. Yalom, Irvin D. *The Gift of Therapy: An Open Letter to a New Generation of Therapists and Their Patients.* Harper Perennial, 2017.

3.4

SHADOW OF LIGHT: FEAR AND DOUBTS

DESCENDING ANOTHER LEVEL DEEPER INTO MY ANGER

My anger was not just silencing my inner child and suppressing my light, it was also covering all my fear and doubts. Because anger was my coping mechanism for protection, I didn't have access to the underlying fears. I wasn't conversing with my fears because I'd been living in anger for so long. My anger said: don't you dare mess with me. My anger existed to cover my deep fear of being messed with. The anger protected me because I wasn't connected to my courage. True courage is entering the arena without armor. We are in the arena not to hurt one another but to love and trust one another. Courage is not the absence of fear but choosing to move forward while looking straight into the eyes of fear and saying *I am choosing to still go through*.

Building my courage step by step was when I took the leap of faith in myself and loosened my tight grasp around my anger while letting other feelings in. I started to see my biggest fears and doubts. Every day is an opportunity to let go of another layer of fear and embrace courage. I will never fully arrive at being completely fearless because growth is always there.

These are my biggest fears: fear of abandonment which is truly a fear of being hurt, fear of relationships ending, fear of losing the people I love, fear of losing myself, fear of being trapped in my darkest shadows, and never being able to get out, fear of failing, fear of succeeding, fear of hurting others, fear of being not good enough, fear of rejection, fear of putting myself out there, fear of having no boundaries, fear of having too rigid of boundaries, fear of being alone, fear of needing others, fear of being too much for others, fear of loving others more than they love me, fear of change, fear of being stuck, fear of trusting others, fear of being poor, fear of being rich, fear of letting go, fear of being vulnerable, fear of regret, fear of judgment, fear of being big, fear of being small, fear of being powerful, fear of being weak, fear of being taken advantage of, fear of being authentic, fear of being truly seen, fear of being misunderstood, and fear of just being me.

SILENCING MY INNER CHILD

In chapter 3.1, I talked about losing my light as I looked into my father's eyes and that I went from child to adult overnight. I learned to suppress my inner child for years, and I would silence her for too long before I met her again. It would take me many years before I reconnected with my light. My inner child was taught to never trust others because of the fear of being hurt. The opposite of fear is trust, and I didn't trust others, but mostly, I didn't trust myself.

Anytime my inner child would try to grab my attention, I would ignore her. Anytime she would speak up, I would shut her down. I would do to myself and my inner child what I was so fearful that others would do to me.

By silencing my inner child, my light would stay extinguished. Even if there were any little spark of light, it would never have enough oxygen to light up. My inner child was trapped and not able to fully express her creativity—her hurt, her pain, her wonder, her awe, and her fears.

What you refuse to look at will always show up again and again. Carl Jung said, "what you resist not only persists but will grow in size." Which has shortened to many, including Oprah, proclaiming, "What you resist persists."

Refusing to look at my fears just made them bigger, also making my anger stronger and louder. All my fears are still present in my life and have given me many opportunities to practice courage. When I was suppressing my fear with anger, I was living in a state of confusion. Even though I still experience confusion, I get to walk closer to clarity.

RECONNECTING WITH MY LIGHT

My journey to finding my light has been long, slow, and treacherous. It would take me almost 16 years from when I first lost my light to finally experiencing the slightest, barely almost there, ray of light that would pierce the darkness. From then on, my light has been found, dimmed, lit up again shining bright, and has gotten very close to being extinguished. My light has been a rollercoaster of being bright as the sun and dark like the night sky. I now know this is part of the Tao and to trust the process. However, my light has grown stronger with consistency with every wound I heal and every death and rebirth I have. Even with waves of how bright my light emanates from my heart's center, it has never been fully extinguished again. Because this was my biggest lesson in finding my light: once you have lost it and re-find it, you will never ever lose it again.

The way I found my light once it was lost has taken many painful excavating journeys—journeys of visiting my inner child, experiencing and honoring my biggest fears, and courageously moving forward even while shaking uncontrollably with doubt. I have breathed through several panic attacks, sobbed in many parking lots, and held myself as I contemplated suicide—the journey to finding my light was learning how to surrender.

There is power in surrendering. By completely surrendering to the process and yelling out JESUS, TAKE THE WHEEL is how I reconnected with my light. I stopped trying to control because control was me getting in my own way. I had to stop planning for every possible outcome or get stuck in ruminating over every single interaction. I fully had to surrender and trust Source, learning that I would *never* know everything.

I do not give up easily, and I used to believe that surrendering equated to giving up and not trying. But surrendering is *releasing* any attachment to control, fear, and outcomes. Surrendering is turning the *fear* of the unknown into *trusting* the unknown. The unknown is where our greatest fears, but also our greatest gifts, lie. In the unknown, we receive the most delicious wisdom and clarity. I am setting an intention of turning my fear of the unknown into the EXCITEMENT of the unknown.

"Don't plan it all. Let life surprise you a little." — Julia Alvarez

---

HOW OFTEN ARE YOU HAVING DINNER WITH YOUR INNER CHILD?

The first time I visited my inner child, she looked scared, incredibly sad, and was shivering from loneliness. From then on, I vowed to protect my inner child forever and be the parent that my inner child never had.

My inner child's home is a beautiful meadow in the middle of a dense, thick forest. The sun's rays are golden yellow, and my inner child's favorite place is to lay on a small hill in the meadow and bask in the warm light. Every time I visit her, she is usually playing or laying in her favorite spot.

Every time I am processing any pain and facing my darkest shadows, I do it all for her. Anytime I feel like it's too difficult to keep going, I think of her. When I learned to let go of anger as my main motivator, *she* became the reason I did all my emotional work.

With every wound I heal and pain I process, my inner child has become less sad, less hurt, and less lonely. With every new visit, we would spend more time playing, giggling, frolicking, and hugging. I would French braid her hair, and we would pick wildflowers and ride horses as fast as we could.

I remember a time when I was having dinner by myself on one of my solo trips, and she appeared. I was sitting in a restaurant with a table full of all the food I over-ordered. I purposefully left my phone in my hotel room and didn't bring a book with me. I wanted to go on a date with myself and enjoy every bite of a delicious feast. As I was savoring the bite of a perfectly flavored mushroom, my inner child appeared and sat across from me. Her feet dangled in the chair she was sitting on, and we shared a wonderful meal together. With sauce dripping down her chin as she grinned through every forkful of tasty food, I delighted in her joy of eating and refusal of using a napkin. She was wild and happy. She could tell I was mulling over something, but instead of saying anything, she just squeezed my hand quickly and disappeared as the waiter brought the check. I was grateful for the dinner we shared and the honor of seeing her grow more sure of herself. That was the first time we got to bond outside of her safe home, and I was grateful for her resiliency.

Since that dinner, every visit to see my inner child has been full of joy but also heart-wrenching love. I don't have children of my own yet, but this is how I imagine mothers must feel when they look at their child: seeing how lovely they are that it melts your heart open so much it aches. There would be times when I would visit my inner child and be afraid that my sadness would rub off on her.

Years after having dinner with my inner child, I had a profound experience during a shamanic journey with Jay. I was having a particularly hard time healing another layer of my deeply triggered abandonment wound, and journeying with Jay as my guide was just what I needed and more. My shamanic journey was full of so many powerful and healing experiences with journeys within the journey, and one of them was a visit with my inner child. As I walked through the thick and dense forest, I approached the clearing and the meadow. There she was, playing in her favorite spot, singing to herself and giggling. I stood at the edge of the meadow, still hidden in the darkness of the forest, as I watched and admired her. My heart was weighted with my love for her, and I was hesitant to say hi or approach her. Jay guided me to ask my spiritual guides for help. I called upon Guan Yin (Kuan Yin) to give me the courage to approach my inner child and not negatively affect her. I took a deep breath and stepped out of the edge of the forest, and quietly said hi as I subtly waved. My inner child perked up and yelled HIIIIIIIIIIIII and furiously waved her hand. With a beaming smile, she jumped to her feet and ran to where I was standing, and gave me a giant hug. She grabbed my hand and tugged me to her favorite spot on the hill of the meadow. She instructed me to lay down, and as I sunk into the soft grass, I felt the warm sun on my face and all over my body. My inner child started putting wildflowers all around the silhouette of my body and interweaved the flowers with my hair. She delightfully laughed with the entirety of her body. Her laughter is the best music I have ever heard, and I am in bliss.

She started to brush my hair with her hands and put my head in her lap. She caressed my face as I cried. She held me in her arms as I wept. She thanked me and told me that because of all my healing work I have been doing, she's been able to be free, happy, and wild. She thanked me for doing the work so that she wouldn't have to be burdened with all the pain that she, as a child, couldn't process. As she held me and hugged me, I felt a love I had never felt before. With past visits, I have held and hugged her, but now my inner child was hugging and holding *me*. She said I didn't need to protect her anymore and that she is no longer fragile.

This moment with my inner child was the most healing and loving experience I have ever had. The times that were too painful to process and overwhelmingly sad were worth it. I will gladly dive into the deepest depths of my despair, knowing that healing is the most loving gift we can give ourselves.

TRUST IS THE ANTIDOTE TO FEAR

Like I said before, I will never be fully absent from fear. Fear is part of being human and protects us from being harmed. Fear alerts us to prepare for the fight, flight, freeze, or fawn response. However, being trapped in debilitating fear because of distrust perpetuates more fear and pain in our lives. With every lesson and experience, I learn to respect my fear but not get stuck in it. I learn to trust myself and others more and more.

I always come back to Winnie's example of trust. The bird on the branch doesn't rely on the branch to never break. Instead, the bird trusts in the ability to use their wings to fly. The bird is not focused on the branch.

I grow closer to letting go of my attachment to my fears when I focus more on my ability to connect to the light within me. I know that I am one prayer or meditation away from the love and protection I need. I get to trust that I will receive clarity and be able to see through the fog of my fears. I am closer to trusting myself, welcoming pain and pleasure equally, trusting the process, and knowing that I will never know more than Source, God, the One, and that I don't ever *need* to know everything.

3.5

SHADOW OF HUMILITY: EGO, ARROGANCE, UNWORTHINESS, JUDGMENT, COMPETITION, AND COMPARISON

THE UNENDING CYCLE OF UNWORTHINESS AND ARROGANCE

I am my harshest critic and judge, and I know I am not alone in this feeling. I have spent most of my life in a cycle of feeling absolute hatred for myself and feeling so unworthy, then not wanting to feel like such trash that I have to be my own hype man and pump myself up to be this amazing person, eventually seeing how I am of course not perfect or amazing and mounting myself off of my own pedestal that I built, and going back to feeling unworthy where the cycle starts all over again. I have learned that this cycle of unworthiness and arrogance will continue forever until I step into the full embodiment of who I am and see that I am no better or worse than anyone.

I have experienced imposter syndrome in every step of my growth. Even in writing this book, I have asked myself, "What qualifies me as an author? Why would anyone want to read what I have to say?" Then I would swing to, "Because I am awesome and magical, that's why!" Both sides are illusions. However, both extremes have some truth. There is some truth to not being qualified—while there is truth that nobody is ever qualified their first time trying something new. Additionally, there is also some truth in that I am magical and awesome. But *everyone* is magical and awesome in their own way. Humility is focusing on our own lane and not ignoring others' paths, but celebrating their journey with the same reverence for your own.

Culturally, I grew up learning that humility was being humble and not accepting praise while lowering oneself to prevent being arrogant. Because of this, I would not believe the compliments I was given while desperately craving the praise and validation I was actively rejecting. I would also be stuck in a place of hierarchy where I would judge and compare myself to others that were "lower" than me while being envious of others that were "above" me. The need for hierarchy is rooted in our capitalistic and patriarchal society that has been drilled into all of us. The ways I have judged others are nowhere compared to how harshly I have judged myself. The ways I have belittled myself to such low levels of unworthiness are some of my deepest shadows that I have barely touched the surface of. I have so much digging and excavating to do, but let me tell you about some that I have started facing.

MY MENTAL AND EMOTIONAL HEALTH

A lot of my unworthiness has been related to my mental health. For most of my life, I have believed that I am stupid because of the messages I received and that my lack of intelligence was the reason for not being able to overcome my mental illness. I learned to take the stigma and internalize it, resulting in shame and self-hatred.

I have been diagnosed with some mental illness that is sometimes used casually in everyday language. People say, "I am so OCD" or "I have such ADHD sometimes," when in reality, they have some obsessions or inattention but nevertheless, they do not have what people in the mental health field call "the criteria to meet the diagnosis." A diagnosis or label can be empowering for some, disempowering for others, and a mix of both empowerment and disempowerment for many. While I don't blame people for saying they have OCD and ADHD when they really don't, and I am not here to be enforcing political correctness, I want to share my story of what it feels like to live with mental illness.

Here are the diagnoses that I have according to the current DSM-5: Obsessive Compulsive Disorder (OCD), Attention Deficit Hyperactivity Disorder (ADHD), Generalized Anxiety Disorder (GAD), and Major Depressive Disorder (MDD). I have been clinically diagnosed with these disorders, and here is my personal experience with having them. I know this is not everyone's experience, and I hope that my story will open understanding in you as you bear witness to my struggle. I want to add that understanding can be expressed in multiple ways. I am fully open to the way someone relates to me and laughs in earnest, head nodding, or feels understood in the ways their OCD or ADHD manifests and feels connected to my story. By unleashing my story, I hope to inspire others to do the same.

CAN'T STOP OBSESSING NO MATTER HOW HARD I TRY

From a young age, I would love to organize Legos into specific categories and colors. I would get extremely upset if any of the other kids at daycare messed up my perfect Lego organization. I loved arranging and constantly rearranging my stuffed animals, sometimes to a point where I would refuse to come to dinner until my stuffed animals felt "just right." I would delight in the ways different colors spoke to me when I colored and how I knew which exact colors would perfectly complement one another. During play time, I would practice fire drills and time myself on how long it would take me to get my most valuable toys into a box and shuck it down the hallway. I had hints of "OCD-like" tendencies growing up, but it wasn't until the divorce that it became debilitating and a full-blown "issue."

OCD is rooted in *extreme* anxiety and difficulty in tolerating uncertainty that gets in the way of daily functioning. Having OCD also comes with the frustrating awareness that some of my obsessions and compulsions don't make any sense, yet I can't stop myself from obsessing or needing to check just *one. more. time.* In the first year living with my dad after the divorce, at ten years old, my obsessive tendencies grew into a clinical level of OCD. I remember I became obsessed with all the doors in the hallway being closed. To this day, I still can't make sense of what I was scared of and what it meant if the doors stayed open, but I would ruminate over needing every single door closed. I would spend a lot of my energy and time tugging on each doorknob to make sure they were closed. Some research shows a possible link between childhood trauma and OCD, but I wonder if I was already predisposed to having OCD before the divorce. I don't fully attribute my OCD to the divorce, but I know it exacerbated it. OCD, for me, manifested as a way to have control because I never felt safe. It was my way of having a sense of control when I was absorbing the chaos in my home as a sensitive child.

It is sometimes hard to explain the way my OCD looks today. Some people have the same obsessions and compulsions throughout their life, but many of my obsessions and compulsions have changed over time. Some of my obsessions and compulsions have been consistent, but some I will outgrow and then be replaced with something new. The International OCD Foundation says this about compulsions: "These are repetitive behaviors or thoughts that a person uses with the intention of neutralizing, counteracting, or making their obsessions go away. People with OCD realize this is only a temporary solution, but without a better way to cope, they rely on the compulsion as a temporary escape. Compulsions can also include avoiding situations that trigger obsessions. Compulsions are time consuming and get in the way of important activities the person values[1]." My OCD has prevented me from being on time to work, school, appointments, etc. because I can't leave my place without checking and rechecking that the stove is off, the lights are off, the heater or AC is off, and no heating pad or blanket is plugged in. I spend a lot of time and energy avoiding trash cans and dumpsters or anything sticky, checking if I touched something dirty and sticky, doubting if the door is really locked, counting and recounting my items, and more. It is so *extremely* exhausting having OCD.

MY ADHD BRAIN

What is more complicated than having OCD is having OCD *and* ADHD. When my OCD brain wants to hyperfocus on checking and rechecking and obsessing, my ADHD brain can't focus on anything. My ADHD brain prevents me from focusing on what is important, and my OCD makes me hyperfocus on what is definitely not important. My OCD makes me late, but my ADHD also makes me have no concept of time. I always think I have 15 more minutes than I really have. I have both attention deficits and hyperactivity, not just one or the other. I sometimes have a big burst of energy, and all I want to do is jump up and down, but when it fades, it goes just as quickly as it came. I can't pay attention to anything unless I either am very passionate about the subject or if I expend all my energy into listening. In my first year of grad school, I would take the longest naps after class because I was unmedicated, and my brain hurt from trying to pay attention.

There was a meditation room on campus, and I went in there to nap and cry.

As a child, I would be so hyper that I couldn't stop jumping in place. My nickname was Jumping Ji or Jumping Bean. I would repeatedly hit my head against the wall when throwing a fit. I would refuse to clean up my toys, promising that I was not done playing even though I would fall asleep five minutes after. I would do my homework as fast as possible because my mom didn't let me play until I was done with my work. I didn't care about any errors or being right. I believed in "done is best." Because of my inability to pay attention and sit still, I would receive messages that I was stupid. I always believed I was stupid and thought I was only smart and capable in specific areas. It was only until my third year of grad school that I finally believed I was not only emotionally intelligent but intelligent in academia as well.

What people don't always know about ADHD is that it doesn't just affect attention in school or work but also in relationships and family dynamics. People with ADHD have different functioning in the prefrontal cortex that not only affects attention but emotional regulation. My romantic relationships have definitely been affected by my inability to always regulate my emotions. When Eric and I first started dating, he couldn't handle my "big" emotions. I would feel rejected and misunderstood, and I blamed him for being out of touch with his emotions as the reason why he couldn't handle my emotions. Although there was some truth to that, there was also truth in my intense emotion filling up the entire space of the relationship leading to him feeling suffocated. I would go through periods of feeling completely out of control.

The combination of having ADHD and OCD can be confusing. I sometimes feel like I am being tugged at both ends in complete conflict. I am impulsive while fearful, compulsive, have trouble focusing while also hyperfocusing, super organized, disorganized, controlling, chaotic, easily overwhelmed, unable to prioritize, over prioritize, detail oriented, big picture focused, and more.

Because of how my OCD and ADHD manifested, it led to anxiety and depression. I get anxious and fearful about how others will judge me if they see me doing my OCD compulsive rituals. My anxiety has peaks and valleys, but it is always present. I have currently been free of depressive symptoms for months. In clinical terms, we say "MDD with remission." However, I want to move away from using the word remission. If my depression comes back, then it comes back. But I don't want to feel like I am in remission, only waiting with a guaranteed promise for my depression to creep back up. For me personally, the word remission in itself is depressing. Depression does not equate to sadness, and I, of course, have felt sadness. Being sad is part of being human. But depression is a heavy weight of persistent sadness that can't seem to stop. I have had periods of deep depression where I feel multiple levels of unworthiness that seem impossible to climb out of. Having OCD and ADHD has contributed to my depression. A lot of my shame and need to hide is because I don't want others to see how ugly I really am. For me, depression feels like I don't want to get out of bed, I want to hide under the covers forever, I am disgusted and ashamed, and I just want to cry and weep until I disappear.

TAKE 'EM IF YOU NEED 'EM

I believe in Western Medicine *and* Eastern Medicine. As a grad school student on my way to getting my psychology degree, there is an emphasis on the scientifically proven medical model. There are some Eastern medicine practices that may not be scientifically proven but have had many more centuries of proven usage than Western medicine practices.

I am a holistic healer, and I live my life holistically. I take psychiatric medicine, and I also take Traditional Chinese Medicine (TCM) herbs. I do not prefer one over the other because both work for me. I believe that hugging a tree can be just as healing as an antidepressant. My philosophy is this: if it works for you, use it.

I used to have a lot of shame about my need for meds. I still struggle with this shame, but it isn't as loud as they first were *before* I started taking medication. I thought I wasn't strong enough because I needed them to function and that there must be something wrong with me if I couldn't live without them. I take Adderall for my ADHD, and I take Lexapro (an antidepressant / SSRI) for my anxiety, depression, and OCD. I understand the consequences of taking medication and that each one will have side effects on my mind, body, and energy. For example, I know that Adderall for my ADHD will sometimes worsen my anxiety and OCD. However, for someone who refused medication for years, the advantages of meds heavily outweigh the disadvantages.

My shame about having ADHD tells me this: You are weak for needing Adderall to get up in the morning so that you don't feel overwhelmed by all the things you need to do in order to get your day started. You are stupid for not being able to pay attention and stay focused in class, meetings, conversations, assignments, projects, and even watching movies. You are "crazy" for not being able to always manage your emotions and for being tugged along by every single emotion you feel. You are incompetent because you are always late and are horrible at managing your time. You cannot be trusted due to being impulsive and for making decisions without proper due diligence. You are not normal, and there is something wrong with you.

My shame about my OCD, anxiety, and depression tells me this: You are weak for needing to be on an antidepressant to function because you are not strong enough to overcome your feelings of worthlessness, your obsessions, and compulsions and you're ruminating and overthinking. Why can't you just snap out of it? You waste so much time obsessing and constantly checking and rechecking with your compulsions just so that you can experience small relief and then go back to doing it *again*. You use so much of your brain power and energy into overthinking and not being able to control your anxiety. Why can't you just let go of all your fears? There must be something wrong with you if you can't let go of all your fears, if you can't just *choose* to be happy, and if you have constant doubt about whether the stove is *really* off or if the door is *actually* locked. You are so weak for depending on meds.

My shame goes through waves of being loud and being quiet as a whisper. What helps is not to try to eradicate the shame and symptoms of my ADHD, OCD, anxiety, and depression, but rather make my self-love and self-compassion louder than the shame.

My self-love and self-compassion tell me this: You are so courageous for taking your meds. You were so afraid of taking medication, and you resisted your need for them for years, but now you are taking them. What an act of self-love! You are asking for help and *receiving* the help. That is radical. Because you are on your meds, you get to really dive deep and look at your wounds so you can heal. Before your meds, you were so afraid of the depths of your depression that you weren't able to always dive deep. You are so brave and courageous. Courage is not the absence of fear. It is acknowledging the fear and still choosing to commit to moving forward. You don't need to let go of all your fears. Your courage muscle is strong, and it gets to grow even stronger as you face each fear. Your ADHD can be hard but look at how creative you are, how joyfully you sing at the top of your lungs, and how distracted you get whenever you see a beautiful tree or flower. You know how to enjoy life's gifts. Your OCD makes the mundane so much fun. You really bask in the satisfaction of playing dishwasher Tetris until all the plates and bowls are perfectly spaced, saving lots of water and electricity. You make sure you and others are safe by washing your hands thoroughly and triple checking that the door is locked. You are not abnormal. You just happen to have a neurodivergent brain living in a neurotypical world. Your anxiety makes you sensitive to stress, which is good for checking in that you are taking care of yourself. Because of your anxiety, you have been diligent in practicing meditation and being present about your breathing. Your anxiety also keeps you safe, being alert about any potential danger. You get to practice self-soothing on a consistent and regular basis. It also has made you empathetic, a strength you need as you move towards becoming a psychologist. Your depression has let you fully bask in joy. You know what it's like to have no energy, nothing to look forward to, feeling hopeless and worthless, and the craving for a long sleep in the safety of your bed. Because of knowing what it's like when moments of joy *do* come, you take full advantage with full gratitude for its presence. You are so strong. You have come so far. You are doing the best you can, and you are able to have so much compassion and love for others as you practice self-love and self-compassion.

With any medication, take 'em if you need 'em. It is an act of radical self-love and self-compassion to take medication. My doctor changes the dosages to my meds depending on if I need more or less. Anytime I needed a higher dosage, I would feel my shame yelling at its loudest level. However, I was also grateful for the opportunity to practice self-love and self-compassion. It takes a lot of courage to ask for help—whether that be for medication, therapy, or other modalities of healing. I am courageous to ask for help even when I sometimes feel frozen and stuck by the weight of mental illnesses. I am thankful for my meds when I take them every morning. I am not worse or better than anyone for needing meds.

BEING NEURODIVERGENT IN A NEUROTYPICAL WORLD

People with ADHD and OCD are seen as having a neurodivergent brain. There are other disorders and conditions that also fall under the category of being neurodivergent. Our patriarchal society and capitalistic world have rewarded productivity, tangible successes, being on time, and measurable goals. It has confused rest with laziness, being different as bad, and creativity with luxury. Being neurodivergent in a neurotypical world has left me feeling punished for not walking in the straight line that others have laid out for me. If the world didn't measure time to the exact second and still used the sun and moon to tell time, I wouldn't be considered late. If society rewarded being creative without any attachment to outcome and encouraged play for the sake of play without purpose, I wouldn't be considered scatterbrained.

I have spent so much time competing and comparing myself to other people. All it did was make me feel like there was something wrong with me. It would push me to grind harder, better, faster, and win. I would spend so much energy hiding my OCD and making sure people didn't think I was stupid. I demanded excellence and would shame myself if I never overcame my unattainable pressure with a huge smile on my face. I understand that there is a human need to compare. Comparison is so ingrained in us and part of our human wiring. Brené Brown, in her book *Atlas of the Heart*[2], says, "More often than not, social comparison falls outside of our awareness - we don't even know we're doing it." We can't help but compare, but we do have a choice in how we relate to the comparisons we make. I learned that competing and comparing the way I have been most of my life is detrimental to my joy. I saw that not having compassion for myself and refusing to accept the reality of my human limitations was preventing me from stepping into my authentic self. I made the choice to no longer grind for my self-worth. Others can't always accept our reality, but we can accept our reality. Others don't have to understand me, but I can understand me.

My ADHD and OCD are the Tao. It is Yin and Yang. As much as I feel conflicted about having both ADHD and OCD, they also balance each other out. When my ADHD wants to cartwheel off into imagination and play at all times, my OCD helps anchor the tasks at hand. When my OCD wants to ruminate and obsess over the same thing, my ADHD helps with letting go of the fixation.

If our society were more compassionate towards people with neurodivergent brains, our world would be a lot more colorful, flexible, kind, slow moving, less wasteful, and fun. There would be an appreciation for beauty in the messiness of living a full human life. I have not waited for society to understand me to start seeing the magical balance of my neurodivergent brain. I know that I get to appreciate my gifts through my imperfections. Curiosity is the antidote to judgment, and I ask this: can we be more curious about ourselves and others rather than jumping straight into assumptions?

THE GIFTS

One of the biggest loving gifts I have given myself is giving up the goal of getting off of meds. I used to spend a lot of energy and time focusing on this goal, but it only perpetuated my shame of needing meds and hindered my growth. By setting the goal of no longer needing medication, I was preventing myself from surrendering to the help that was being given to me. I asked for help, and here it was. This is what I know: I need my meds right now, and they are such a blessing. Maybe I won't need them in the future, but that is not my focus. I am not looking into tomorrow. I am saying today, in my present moment, the meds help, and I am gladly taking them.

The biggest gift of my ADHD is the discovery of my crayons. My partner Eric first coined the term crayons because he once said, "Your brain is like a box of melted crayons." He meant that because of my wacky creativity and need to play constantly—there are crayons living in my brain. I am a crayon, the crayons are in me, and it is very meta. The crayons are hilarious because they love finishing sentences, even though they rarely make sense. The crayons *absolutely love* trees, flowers, plants, dogs, squirrels, disco balls, shiny twinkling lights, sequins, and bright colors. They have a horrible memory and are constantly playing a game of telephone from one ear to another, eventually leading to mistaken associations and mixed-up meanings. For example, I swear I heard Eric say I could have the rest of the pie, but in "reality" he said I could have a piece of the pie. The crayons put the quotes around reality. They are mischievous and are constantly dancing. They are always scheming for sugar and love playing. I get to appreciate my crayons because they are rooted in creativity. I am easily distracted into playing, and most times of the day, I choose to play and be creative instead of getting work done. And this is also why I am thankful for my OCD for helping me get my crayons in line when needed. Having crayons has helped me have more compassion for my brain and my ADHD. It has also helped Eric be more patient with my constant forgetfulness and tardiness. I have only explained a small snippet of the magic of my crayons and for a masterclass on understanding my crayons, talk to Eric.

I get to step into my full embodiment and my full expression of the Tao. Instead of seeing what is wrong with me, I get to see the perfection of my brain. I am made perfectly imperfect, and I get to practice being grateful for therapy, acupuncture, Reiki, herbs, medication, nature, and more for supporting me at all times. I get to graduate from the patriarchal need to compare and compete with others and make conscious choices on how I will react to my human wired comparing ways. I get to let go of my impossible perfect idealized self. I get to fully appreciate my anxiety, depression, ADHD, and OCD. I get to see how perfect we all are and that everyone is their expression of the Tao.

---

1. https://iocdf.org/about-ocd/
2. Brown Brené. *Atlas of the Heart: Mapping Meaningful Connection and the Language of Human Experience.* Random House Large Print, 2022.

3.6

SHADOW OF HARMONY: DRAMA SEEKING AND CONFLICT CREATING

LIFE'S SOURNESS

Here is the part where I write about my relationship with my dad and how much I avoided talking about it, looking at it, and sharing about it. I could barely even tell Winnie as I choked through my tears and words. I desperately want an intimate and loving relationship with my dad. If I don't release this resentment and pain I've been holding onto for so long, I won't be able to have the relationship I want with him.

Maybe my sister and I are so close because we are also trauma bonded by being the only ones to experience and witness the full dumpster fire of our parents' divorce. My sister and I held on to each other for dear life because if we didn't rely on each other, we were *all* going to die. We are still holding hands with each other through everything. We are each other's life rafts.

I have talked at length about my anger towards my mom, but I haven't really spoken about my anger towards my dad. When we arrived in Salinas from Texas, my dad was such a mess. He was chain-smoking packs of cigarettes, and his anger was oozing out of him. I get it. My mom left a note on the kitchen counter telling my dad she wanted a divorce and then she ran away. That was how she told him. She never gave him a chance to talk or express his side. Part of my anger towards my dad is that he took all his hurt and rage at my mom and took it out on my sister and me. Hurt people hurt people, and he was extremely hurt, and he would rage so hard at us.

What my mom doesn't fully know to this day is how much my dad hurt my sister and me. Anytime my sister and I asked him if we could see our mom, he would beat us. He would say, how dare we ask him that. His go-to spanking tool was a plastic clothing hanger. He would hit my sister and me with it until the hanger broke, and then it was done. I longed and wished for the hanger to break quickly every time he hit us.

He even changed the home phone number on my mom. He knew I was talking to her daily, and I didn't have a cell phone. He changed the number, thinking it would cut off communication, but I laughed at him, telling him he wasted his money because I would just tell mom the new number. That laugh also resulted in a beating.

My sister and I handled our parents' divorce differently. She threw herself into school and extracurriculars. She was going to bolt out of this hellhole and work hard to go to college. I threw myself into being the glue, trying to hold everyone together. I would spend hours talking on the phone with my mom and spend hours with my dad once he got home from work. We would play chess with no strategy, just moving the pawns and bishops around while I asked him questions and talked to him. I was his mini therapist without knowing I was playing that role. That was how I found out about my mom leaving a letter on the kitchen counter for him to read when he got home from work. It is also how I learned that when he first got home from work that night, he didn't see the letter and assumed she was at our neighbor's house. When he got to the neighbor's house, Mom's Dude's ex-wife was there too, and my dad learned that she got discarded the same way.

Because of the time I spent with my dad, I would eventually be the one to ask our dad if my sister and I could see our mom. The chance of us getting hit was less if I asked rather than my sister. The first year of living with our dad, we only saw our mom once. We got to see her over Thanksgiving in Texas. I remember my sister and I making cinnamon rolls and sharing them with our dad, and finally, I asked, "Can we go visit mom for Thanksgiving?" I braced myself for a potential hit. Instead, he sat there quietly and eventually said yes. A huge wave of relief washed over my sister and me, but we hid our excitement so that he wouldn't grow angry and change his mind.

Thanksgiving came around, and my sister and I were getting to see our mom. The place my mom and Mom's Dude were renting was bigger than what they needed, with enough space for my sister and me too. There was no furniture. A rug in the living room, a dinner table, and only beds in the bedrooms. It was heartbreaking to see all of my mom's grief and hope in all the empty space.

My dad's only rule about us visiting our mom was that Mom's Dude could not be there. I don't know how it was for my sister, but for me, it was hard spending time with our mom. I could see the sadness on her face, and I saw through her attempt at putting a livelier mask on to try to shield us from her pain. I don't have many memories of that trip except sad ones. On Thanksgiving Day, Mom's Dude came by just to drop off some food, and he left. We barely had any interaction with him. When my dad called to check in on my sister and me, he asked us if Mom's Dude had come by. I casually told my dad that he had come by to drop off some food but left.

Later, I saw my mom crying, and quickly I realized what had happened. My dad was angry with her for not following his only rule: Mom's Dude was not to be there with us. I didn't know that I was supposed to lie when my dad asked. I didn't know I was being tested. I was eleven years old that Thanksgiving. I didn't learn the loving benefit of a white lie until that day. My sister and I wouldn't see my mom again for the rest of that school year. That would be the last time we would go to Texas. I blamed myself for my sister's and my separation from our mother. I believed that if I had just lied to my dad, that maybe we would've seen her more than just that one time that whole year. I still carry the shame to this day. As I write this, I am still in so much pain.

I understood my dad's anger and fear. He had one rule, and it wasn't *technically* kept. He probably also believed that there was a risk of us not coming back. Maybe my mom would try to prevent us from returning home to Salinas.

After that first year of living in Texas, my mom and Mom's Dude would move to southern California. It was in the hopes that because she would be only a six-hour drive away from us, rather than a plane ride away from us, maybe she could see us more.

Some of my saddest memories take place at the middle of nowhere truck stops. This is because sometimes, my mom would drive five to six hours just to spend time with my sister and me for an hour. My dad would drop us off at a Denny's or McDonald's in the middle of King City or a random truck stop further out. Then my mom would come, and we would eat for an hour before our dad picked us up again. We had one hour with our mom. I could see the sadness and desperation in my mom's eyes. She would ask us to tell her everything about how school was going and anything about our friendships. But I didn't know what to say to her. What could I say in this one hour we have together when all I can see is the sadness behind her eyes?

I didn't know what to say because as I looked into her eyes and saw her sadness and agonizing pain, I felt the guilt and shame of being the source of her sadness. I was the source of her pain. I was responsible for her sadness—because she wasn't the chosen parent. How could I cause her all this pain when I loved her so much? How could a daughter alienate her mother?

This is why I was angry at my dad and avoided it. To look at my anger towards my dad, I would also have to look at the pain I gave my mom. I was on team dad in my mother's eyes and on team mom in my father's eyes. I held on to my anger towards my mom because Mom's Dude was the easy scapegoat, and she was in a relationship with him. But I was in denial about how angry I was at my dad, avoiding, avoiding, avoiding. By persistently avoiding, I was creating conflict with my dad, but also internal conflict within myself. When I looked at my anger towards my mom, I saw how I hurt my dad every time I asked him to see our mom. Each parent felt alienated when all I did was try to be a loving daughter to both of them.

TURNING LEMONS INTO LEMONADE

How I forgive my mom and dad is how I forgive myself. I did my absolute best that I could at ten years old, eleven years old, and so on until now. My mom did her absolute best, and she is currently doing the best she can. My dad did his absolute best, and he is also currently doing the best he can. Nobody wakes up with the intent to hurt others. We all wake up just *doing our best*.

My dad deeply hurt my sister and me. But he also loved us fiercely. After a year and a half of living with him, when I told him over another game of chess that he needed to stop smoking and stop taking his anger out on my sister and me, he stopped. My dad was so hurt by the way my mom left him, and he was in the depths of his pain, not able to see beyond it. I don't blame him. I can't. He was single-parenting while mourning and raging. What my dad taught me was his ability to forgive. He forgave my mom before I got to a place to forgive her. My dad also taught me the healing gift of humor. He has the ability to laugh through pain in ways that are pure magic. He also was a single dad who raised my sister and me during our hardest times—when we were in the worst parts of puberty. He isn't a perfect dad, but I am so grateful for his ability to *show* up, with his flaws and all.

My dad is the first one to say I love you and the first one to say I'm sorry. He is the funniest man I know and has made my sister and I howl with laughter more times than he hurt us. He is a dad who is not afraid to cry. I have seen my dad cry more times than I've seen other men in my life cry. He has also loved us more than he has hurt us. My dad has taught me the magical medicine of laughter and joy. I am grateful for this opportunity to heal another layer of pain and move forward in welcoming my dad into my heart.

With all the lemons I was given by my mom, dad, and the universe, I have turned them into the sweetest tasting lemonade. What is even better is knowing that I am not finished using all the lemons. There is always more lemonade to be made.

TASTING SWEET SUGAR

Some stories that paint the perfection of my dad, doing his best as a single-parent:

When I first thought I got my period (my hymen broke when I was attempting the splits), he came home with balloons and a cake that said

"Happy Woman Day!" It was one of those classic red strawberry glazed topped cakes you get at the grocery store, and it was to celebrate that I was now a woman. I have a dad that celebrated his daughter getting a period, rather than one who would run away at the mere thought of his daughter being a "woman."

One time, my dad was driving my sister and me around, and we were at the height of our feelings being teenage girls. We were both just nagging and whining at our dad and being ruthlessly mean because our feelings were *so big* while going through puberty. The yelling got too loud for him during the drive, and he drove into the nearest gas station. He got out of his car to put gas in, and while I was inside the car sitting in the backseat near the car's fuel tank, I heard the loudest sigh come out of his mouth. He didn't need gas. He just needed a break. And the only break he could get from us was putting gas in the car. When he got back in the car, I started crying and saying how sorry I was for being mean. That I have all these feelings and I don't know what to do with them. Then he started crying, and all he could say was *thank you, thank you* through his tears.

Another time, my sister ditched school and went to Target. She ran into our dad there. He asked her, "Aren't you supposed to be in school?" She replied with, "Aren't you supposed to be at work?" He acknowledged her point. He then quickly asked if she wanted to go watch a movie together.

3.7

SHADOW OF FLOURISHING: LACK AND SCARCITY MINDSET

For most of my childhood, my dad was a small business owner selling shoes and clothing. As an immigrant, he had few options for work so his only choice was to have a small business, but my dad liked being his own boss. Shoes were his main bread and butter. He would sell all types of sneakers: Jordans, Air Force 1s, Air Maxes, Cortezes, Chuck Taylors, Puma classics, Adidas Superstars, Stan Smiths, and more. Growing up, he had a couple of stores in indoor swap meets in Salinas and a standalone store in King City called Shalom Town. I grew up playing in swap meets, eating delicious tortas followed by a chaser of Mexican candies that have a perfect combination of spicy and sweet. I would ride the coined operated horse, while my mom would keep feeding the machine with coins so I could continually ride. She would always have to warn me when it was going to be the last ride because I would throw a fit every *single* time my turn was over. I was unfazed and completely unconcerned about the other kids and their parents waiting patiently for their turn.

As classic 90's and early 2000's kids, my sister and I wore all the sneakers. My mom would dress us from head to ankle, and my dad would dress our feet. This meant that we would wear our school uniforms, have butterfly glittered clips in our hair, stockings on, and then have Allen Iverson's Reebok sneakers or Nike Air Force 1s on our feet. I still laugh about the mental portraits of my sister and me in our eclectic fashion.

BREWING FINANCIAL TROUBLES

By the time our mom and dad divorced, our dad had one store. He had sold the swap meet businesses and kept the store in King City. We lived in Salinas, but he would do one-way hour-long drives back and forth to King City. While living with my dad after the divorce, he started having financial troubles. The business wasn't doing so well, bills were piling up, and he was single parenting. We were personally experiencing the beginning hints of the economy slowing down that would eventually lead to the financial crisis of 2008.

In 2005, our dad told my sister and me his plans to move to Portland, Oregon, for a business opportunity there. My sister was almost done with high school, and I was finishing up middle school. By the timing of Portland, my sister would probably be off to college, and I would be in high school. Because I knew I wanted to go to art school in California, I didn't want to move to Portland because I wouldn't be able to get California state grants for college if I graduated high school in another state. That was when I asked my dad if it was okay to live with mom since she now lived in Los Angeles, and I could get a high school degree in California. He said yes because, by this time, my dad softened about our connection with our mom.

In the summer of 2006, I moved to Burbank to live with my mom and Mom's Dude. I would start as a freshman in high school that year, and it was my first year living apart from my sister. My sister stayed in Salinas that year to finish her senior year of high school. Although my sister and I are four years apart, we are three grades apart in school. That freshman year was hard. I missed my sister and dad desperately. I was happy to live with my mom again, but being without my sister for the first time broke my heart. Part of the shame and guilt I still hold onto is for feeling like I abandoned my sister and dad by leaving.

Another big part of my shame is that the year we lived apart, the financial troubles were some of the biggest, and I wasn't there to hold my sister's hand. Our dad was trying to sell our house to prevent bankruptcy and to have money for the business in Portland. The house would not sell and eventually foreclosed, he lost his business in King City, and his Portland business opportunity fell through. That year was hard for my sister and dad and me. I was missing them and feeling shame for not being there for them while they were dodging calls from collectors. I wasn't there when my sister's car got repossessed or when the house had to be emptied for the bank. My dad eventually declared bankruptcy, and I still feel shame for not being able to hug him through it all.

My sister eventually moved to Burbank so that she could go to college while living at home. We only lived apart for one year, but our reunion was so sweet and needed. I was so happy that my sister and I were living together again. We even shared a bedroom, and I would go to sleep happy knowing that my sister was right next to me.

After declaring bankruptcy and the Portland business opportunity falling through, our dad also eventually moved to Southern California. His sisters and brothers lived in the Cerritos area, and he lived with them until he got back on his feet. With my sister and now dad living closer to me, I never went back to Salinas. I never got to say goodbye to the home we lost, where some of our happiest memories and biggest heartbreaks were experienced. I never got to walk around my neighborhood for the last time to say bye to the street I grew up on. I never got to fully thank the town of Salinas for being the home that raised me and the place where community was sewn, with a never-ending common thread, into the fabric of our lives.

ALWAYS FEELING POOR

The heartbreaking loss of a hometown is part of my financial trauma. From then on, I felt poor not only in money but also in feeling like I had lost too much. I lost the home I grew up in, a hometown, a community, and a foundation. I could not lose so much ever again, so money became my goal in buying safety and comfort. I wanted to be rich so that I could never lose and be hurt again. In my mind, money was going to save me from my deepest pains. Feeling like I was always lacking in groundedness and comfort cemented in me, and I would look at everything from a scarcity mindset. Being rich was a need to survive. I believed I could also save my mom, dad, and sister from their pains by being rich.

This is where I confused having a strong work ethic as working hard without resting. I started to believe that needing rest was a sign of weakness. I became ambitious for all the wrong reasons. I became perfectionistic, and instead of painting and drawing for the fun of it, I started to try to extract monetary success from my art. After high school, I majored in Advertising at Art Center College of Design because it was a way I could design and make money. I would follow dollar signs and suppress any craving to follow inspiration first. Art Center also measured success in what you produce in your work, further establishing my messed up mindset of only being worthy if I produced tangible success.

I only felt a sense of worth if I could design well and make a living doing it. I felt shame for not making enough money to pay for my student loans and help my parents. I felt less than for not being able to afford what my peers could. I felt embarrassed about my credit card debt and my inability to save money. If my mom or dad *could* give my sister and me money, I know they would. It broke my parents' hearts that they couldn't pay for our college. I didn't want my dad to feel shame about his bankruptcy, so I would never ask him for money. I didn't want my mom to stress about money, so I never asked her for money. The poorest I felt was when I had to choose between buying tampons or putting gas in the car. I put gas in the car so that I wouldn't miss class. I no longer wanted to feel poor, and all my energy went into either working or avoiding any financial shame triggers.

RELEASING MY OWN TRAP

After years of not looking at my financial trauma, I finally started to discuss it in therapy with M. I realized that my parents never put pressure on me to provide for them or save them from their pain. I put that pressure on myself. I built my own trap and put myself in it. I was holding resentment and anger towards my parents for not being able to provide financially when they provided me with unconditional love and empowered me. I was the only one getting in the way of myself, and I hated how cold and money hungry I became.

Nobody cares how rich you are or all the stuff you acquire. I learned to reframe my relationship with money. I started to see money as a tool that you need to pay for bills and for a roof over your head, but that it is nothing more than a tool. Money does not provide self-worth. It does not make me better or less in value than anyone. Money doesn't bring you more love, joy, connection, or understanding. I falsely believed that money would solve all my problems. Thank God I never won the lottery because it would've been harder to learn my lesson. I started reflecting on the ways that I could shift from a scarcity mindset to an abundance mindset.

SCARCITY MINDSET HURTS EVERYONE

Our capitalistic society has indoctrinated the message that there are only enough pieces of pie, and you have to fight to get your own. This concept of "not enough space" is deeply bred by a pervasive lack mentality and scarcity mindset. Society has reared everyone to have this mindset.

With this mindset prevalent in society, it creates a hierarchy. It shows us that some people are at the top, and some are at the bottom. Then each individual assesses and sees how alike or different they are from the people at the top or bottom and figures out where they land. The more scarce your mindset is, *every* interaction and experience is measured against how close in proximity you are to people at the top and how distanced you are from people at the bottom. The scarcity mindset also breeds comparison and competition.

I understand that there is some truth to a lack mentality because there are everyday examples of scarcity. We have a housing crisis, there is a limit to natural resources, there is only so much land and fresh water, and more. However, this is also due to the greediness that is rewarded in our capitalistic society. There are individuals and groups of people that take more than they need and hoard, afraid that someone will take what is "theirs" and still live a life rooted in scarcity. The truth is that many of us have more than enough, and there is plenty to go around and share.

The scarcity mindset creates people to have survival responses, but each individual's response may vary. People can have survival responses in finances, careers, romantic relationships, family dynamics, friendships, and more. The survival response can be staying in an unhappy relationship because "there are no more good ones out there." Another survival response can be overworking because there is only one promotion, and you *must* get it. These survival responses hurt everyone, even people at the top, but it especially hurts people in marginalized communities with multiple intersecting identities.

For example, let's say there is an underserved community that is full of undocumented first-generation immigrants—the people in the community are mostly people of color, the predominant language is not their first language, they are underpaid, the education system is not the best, there is very little access to healthy food and access to healthcare, and parents have to work multiple jobs to make ends meet. In this community, maybe some people "make it out." The person that makes it out is seen as exceptional and rare. This person becomes a token, and there is a high cost to being seen as rare. On the one hand, it can feel good to be praised for hard work and can be inspiring because it may encourage others in the community. On the other hand, it can be toxic because it adds more stress and pressure to not fail. Additionally, a person "making it" doesn't change the oppressive dynamic that still exists in the community. There are still going to be more people who will be stuck in the cycle of oppression than those who experience liberation. Also, the person who makes it doesn't always stay part of the community because they have to leave to go out and "do better things." They may have no choice but to leave because there are more resources and opportunities outside of the community, which can be a loss to both the community and the person leaving.

There are many stories like this where one must leave their home to be able to "succeed." But I ask, what is the definition of success? I want to live in a society that has a more open view on defining success. I don't want success to be *only* measured by the promotions, accolades, wealth, or material affluence. I also want success to be defined by how many times one tapped into the courage to open their heart back up again after feeling rejected or experiencing heartbreak. I also want success to be measured by how much one showed up to the arena after processing their wounds over and over again. I also want success to be determined by how loving and supportive one is for themselves and others.

I'M ALREADY RICH

Being so stuck in my lack mentality and shame, I failed to see how wealthy I already was. I am so rich in relationships, connections, love, and more. I have a loving mom who is strong, tender, resourceful, and present. I have a hilarious dad that is loving, joyful, and easy going. I have an amazing sister that is intelligent, kind, witty, and rooted. I have strong bonds and friendships with so many people that are true treasures in my life. I have so much wealth in my health. I don't have chronic pain or any major medical issues. I get to have an education as I work towards finishing my doctoral degree. I am rich in emotional support from my loved ones. I have so much joy, and I am rich in my relationship with my inner child. I am in abundance with my connection to Source and my Spiritual Guides.

Money can never buy the richness and abundance I already have in my life. The sisterhood bonds can never be bought. The love I get to share with the beautiful people in my life can never be purchased. I am already flourishing, and all it took was letting go of my survival and lack mindset. The shadow of flourishing is not being able to see how rich we already are. I have so much abundance, and I am already sharing my abundance of joy, love, education, connections, relationships, and more. What I receive freely, I promise to also give freely.

3.8

SHADOW OF GRATITUDE: TAKING EVERYTHING FOR GRANTED

엄마, 배고파! (MOM, I'M HUNGRY!)

I can never fully capture the kindness and tenderness of my mom. She shares her love for me and my sister all out in the open. She never holds back on showing us how much she loves us. The handmade birthday cards she gives us every year are the best gifts for the heart and soul. Her favorite words to hear from me are 엄마, 배고파! (Mom, I'm hungry!) I tell her I love her, but telling her I'm hungry is how I say I love her, *and* with the added bonus of, can you love me back?

While living apart from my mom for three years, she didn't get to feed me her delicious meals filled with love three times a day with snacks in between. My dad is a great cook, but with him working most of the day, I didn't have a consistent eating schedule. I was young and didn't know the importance of meals. I only ate when I was hungry, which led to me to losing a lot of weight that first year of living with my dad. It also didn't help that with puberty right around the corner, I shot up three inches in one year, and all my weight went into my height. I could see the pain behind my mom's eyes as I shrank into almost nothingness and the added heartbreak of her not being able to do anything about it. On our daily phone calls, she would ask what I ate that day, and I would get annoyed at having to tell her that I only ate some rice crispy treats and an apple. I took for granted how much my mom loved me by checking in on my eating habits, continuing to ask even while knowing that she would hurt every single time she heard the answer.

Later, when I ended up moving in with her in high school, my mom would constantly feed me, and I started to gain weight. Color returned back to my face. I remember being upset that I was gaining weight, wanting so badly to look like the models in Vogue. I took her cooking, food, and love for granted. Looking back, I was wilting, and she brought me back to life with every nourishing spoonful of rice and kimchi.

Today, when I come to visit her and yell 엄마, 배고파! (Mom, I'm hungry!), my mom is *delighted* to feed me. It doesn't matter if it is 11 P.M. or 7 A.M. If I am hungry, she loves feeding me. It's healing for the both of us. She gets to feed me all the meals she couldn't when I wasn't living with her, and I get to eat all the meals that my younger self craved. It is rare to have a mom that *loves* feeding her children and doesn't see it as a chore. It is a gift to have a mom that thanks *me* just because I eat her food when I should be thanking her. I have taken my mom for granted as I have normalized and expected my mom to cook for me. It's only when Eric or other friends come to my mom's and get fed that I see that I have a special mom.

I have taken my mom's unconditional love for granted. All the years I threw anger and rage at her, she loved me with her full heart and being and never wavered. She made it safe for me to be completely mad at her and hate her because, deep down, I knew I could. I knew she wouldn't stop loving me no matter how much I rejected her. My mom taught me the lessons in understanding unconditional love between a mother and a daughter.

My mom has shown the true meaning of joy. I am only joyful because my mom is the *full* embodiment of joy. She gets so much joy from the littlest of things: seeing a bird perched on her favorite tree, the sun streaming through the windows, and a cup of instant ramen. Even when she is hurting or sad, she can clearly see through her tears and be thankful for the lesson.

Although I share with my mom how much I love her and how grateful I am for her, I can still never thank her enough. Even if I spent all my waking hours thanking my mom, it would still never be enough. My mom has given me life and has also given me creativity, joy, and love. We are in a forever soulful dance.

우리 아빠 (OUR DAD)

I can never thank my dad enough. Growing up, I never knew how different my dad was compared to other dads. My sister and I grew up seeing our dad be honest, funny, and real. To this day, my dad has cried more than any other man I know. I have witnessed my dad cry more than my mom. Our dad told my sister and me he loved us all the time. He never held back and was never afraid to be vulnerable. Growing up with an emotional and open dad is rare, and I took him for granted.

Our dad never believed in the hierarchy that boys were above girls. He raised my sister and me with no assumptions on how girls should be. He treated us the same as he would treat the sons in our small Korean community. Our dad was everyone's dad. If someone was in a fight with their dad, they knew they could talk to my dad.

Just as I took my mom's love and cooking for granted, I have also taken my dad's cooking for granted. My dad is 100% quality over quantity. He doesn't cook many things, but the five to six things he does cook are the best of the best. While living with him, he would make his delicious food, but I would not eat his food. I would get bored of his food since he would cook those meals consistently. I took for granted how much love he put into his cooking. Just like my mom felt pain seeing me lose weight, my dad did too. I was withering away while rejecting his delicious meals.

Although my dad had financial troubles, I took for granted how much he worked to put a roof over my head. He shielded my sister and me from his finances to protect us for as long as he could. He never tried to burden us with any financial issues, and I took his hard work for granted. I blamed him for my financial trauma when in reality, we were so rich in love and support.

Our dad taught my sister and me the gift of 눈치 (noonchi or nunchi). Nunchi is a Korean concept of being able to read social cues, others' moods, and have perfect timing. Nunchi takes high emotional intelligence and is seen as having social common sense. Our dad has high nunchi—being able to read a room quickly and still be authentic. He doesn't shapeshift and mold himself to the situation but rather knows how to disarm any tension quickly with his contagious humor. Nunchi is not easily taught, and my dad gave my sister and me so much nunchi. By being his authentic self, we absorbed his nunchi. We were breathing his qi (chi), and I took him for granted.

My dad loves me so much, and I have spent years denying myself from his love. I can't thank him enough for all the ways he loves me, even when I am being stubborn or harsh. He has listened to all my crap and has never shut me down. I can never fully express how much he means to me.

THE BEST 언니 (OLDER SISTER)

My sister has done so much for me just by existing, yet she still has supported me beyond comprehension. Our mom has told us countless times that my sister was so excited for me to arrive. She had no sibling jealousy, and when I came home from the hospital, my sister looked at me with loving fascination. My sister still looks at me with that loving sister gaze full of wonder.

Growing up, my sister always shared with me. Even though I would be selfish with my toys or presents, my sister gladly gave me everything of hers. She never held back and was always kind and patient. When others would complain that I could be a brat, my sister would respond, "First of all, only I can call her a brat. Also, I know she is a brat, but I love her for it." My sister has fiercely defended me even when I have not deserved it. She has been my protector, and I haven't thanked her enough for doing so.

My sister also taught me to love reading. When we were younger, she would constantly read to her stuffed animals and me. I usually hated reading because my ADHD brain couldn't pay attention long enough. However, my sister read the best stories to me. She would carefully curate the books for play time, picking the ones she knew I would resonate with. If it weren't for my sister, I would have missed out on the love I have for books and reading.

My sister is extremely intelligent, and I know that I am intelligent because I had her as my sister. The gift of my sister's intelligence is that she never made me feel stupid in comparison. Others would compare my sister and me, highlighting how smart she is and highlighting how inadequate I am compared to her. But my sister *never* looked at me as stupid. When I learned to internalize that I am stupid, my sister always rooted me on and shown to me how intelligent and capable I am. I stood in pride, knowing that I must be smart if my sister thinks I am. It is her confidence in me that slowly built the confidence I have in myself. It is through her eyes that I was able to finally let go of the narrative that I am stupid.

My sister inspires me every single day. She went to law school not to become a successful attorney but to become a civil rights attorney. She made the conscious decision to use all her strengths to fight the Goliaths and redistribute power in our society. Every day she chooses to serve the underdogs and give voice to the voiceless. If it weren't for her brave choice to go to law school, I wouldn't have given myself the permission to go to grad school for psychology. She showed me her way so I could do it my way.

In any chaos, my sister can remain calm and steady. Because of her ability to be calm, I have been able to burst into anger, confusion, and fits of rage. I have been allowed to express all my emotions because of my sister's patience and groundedness. With her steadiness, she gives me permission to ride every emotional wave to its end. I can never thank her enough for her endless sacrifices.

Like I expressed earlier in Chapter 3.1, my sister is my favorite person, and I am blessed to have a sister like her in my life. There are not enough words in all the languages combined to express the magnitude of my gratitude to her. I will be forever thankful for her, and even forever will never be enough.

MY GUIDES AND TEACHERS

I would not be here today if it weren't for the teachers and guides I have had in my life journey so far. I am so grateful for all my guides in this human realm and the ones in the spiritual realm. I know that there are guides and teachers that I haven't met yet, and I am looking forward to the time when we will meet. The selfless love and guidance that my teachers and mentors have given me are treasures that I can never repay. They are priceless gold that I can never show enough gratitude for.

I started going to therapy with Jenna, and after two years with her, she recommended me to my current therapist M. Jenna planted so many seeds in me that didn't bloom until later with M. She would plant insights and nuggets of wisdom that I wouldn't wake up to until years later. I thank her for believing in me and holding so much space for me. She didn't get to witness the blooms of the seeds she planted, and I hope this book is a way to honor those seeds. If it weren't for Jenna's unwavering kindness and patience, I would have never continued therapy. Jenna was the first therapist I ever went to, and I didn't know it at the time, but it is truly rare to meet a therapist you connect with on the first try. She was a true blessing from Source.

I've been in therapy with M for almost seven years now. Words cannot capture the amount of loving space M has held for me and continues to hold for me to this day. For the many years I was raging, M saw in me what I couldn't see in myself. M believed in my potential for growth and honored me where I was at. M has been witness to my shadow work, seen me at my worst, and never shied away from my darkest parts even when I wanted to run away from myself. M has guided me in some of the most treacherous paths on my journey and has been my biggest cheerleader. M has opened up so many windows in my heart and doors on my path to becoming a healer. I would have never decided to become a guide and healer myself if it wasn't for M, and I am so grateful. M is still my therapist, and has taught me the limitless healing that can happen with the strong bond of the therapeutic relationship. I am forever grateful to M, not only in this lifetime but past and future lifetimes.

Winnie Chan Wang, my loving and inspiring co-author of this book has also been a big part of my healing journey. She has been a mentor, guide, teacher, and sister to me since the first time we met. I first went to her for acupuncture and reiki energy healing, and now I have the greatest honor of being her soul sister friend and so much more. If it weren't for Winnie, this book would not exist. She has been open and loving towards me, always empowering me to be the healer I am meant to be. She inspires me every single day by being her fullest expression of the Tao, as she honors my fullest expression of the Tao. Winnie is part of my soul family, and I am so grateful for her presence in my life. To try to capture my love and reverence for Winnie is an unattainable goal. There is a constant mutual exchange of love, energy, vulnerability, growth, and liberation between us, and I can't thank her enough for opening her heart to me. Our sisterhood is so healing, and I like to think that before we became human beings, our souls made a friendship pact to meet one another in this current lifetime.

At the same time, I started going to Winnie, and I also started seeing Christina Ledoux. Christina is not only a loving and warm Acupuncturist and Reiki Energy healer, she is also a friend that I get to share Korean roots with. I am always thankful for my and Christina's Korean shamanic bonds and the way she incorporates her connection in her healing. She has opened many paths of healing for me, and I am grateful to her for being an example of how to be in flow. Her way of using sound and frequencies to heal has been truly inspiring to experience. I am eternally grateful to Christina for helping me connect to my spiritual guides and for holding space for me as I process parts of my journey. To be in Christina's warmth and energy is to be kissed with blessings over and over again.

Jay Dubois is a shamanic healer and has helped me go deep in my journeys. He has helped me cultivate stronger relationships with my spiritual guides but has also aided me in journeying to meet my darkest shadows. He has guided me in processing some of my deepest fears and shame. I am grateful to Jay for holding space for me and also for the common themes we share in our deep wounds. Jay's experience of his anger has also helped me in my relationship with my anger. I am deeply grateful to him for helping me excavate and process my wounds. To be the recipient of Jay's openness and honesty is a gift that keeps giving. His presence in itself has been healing in countless ways.

My 할머니, grandmother from my dad's side is one of my spiritual and ancestral guides. She passed away years ago, and we weren't close in this human realm, but we are close in the spiritual realm. She has shown up in many experiences, and I hear her voice at times, especially when I need to pay attention to something. My dad is hilarious, but he has nothing on my grandmother. He got his humor from her, and she is the ultimate matriarch of funny. She has made me laugh through some of my deepest pains, and I am grateful to her for turning my hurt into joy. I can never thank her enough. My grandmother has protected me, guided me, and humored me in more ways than I am aware of. She does it without any expectation, and her watchful presence has been all the medicine I need. I only exist because I have been blessed by her loving embrace. I am honored to be her granddaughter, and multiple lifetimes of gratitude still won't be enough to capture how thankful I am.

Oprah Winfrey doesn't know me, but she has been my teacher and has taught me so much. Her deep and soothing voice is a healing balm for my soul. I have read and listened to her book *What I Know For Sure* numerous times, and each cycle has come with *more* deepening, *more* awakening. When she sings *highhhh vibrationsssss*, it warms me to my bones every single time. I wish that Oprah could read all the audiobooks in the universe or be the new voice of Siri. Oprah has been my companion through many of my awakenings and aha moments. She is a gift and a blessing for sharing Super Soul Sundays, giving more people access to spiritual connection. She made deep reflection and learning mainstream, and I can't thank her enough for all her interviews and all her personal sharing.

THANKFUL FOR MYSELF

As much as I cannot express enough gratitude for others, I cannot express enough gratitude for myself. I can't thank myself enough for how committed I am to healing and growth. I can't thank myself enough for how much I have shown up for myself and for others. I can't appreciate my crayons and my creativity enough. I can't appreciate my joy and ability to always look for the silver linings enough. I can't thank my body enough for all that it does, being my home in this lifetime. I have taken myself for granted constantly, and I have made an intention to be more thankful for myself.

I thank myself for being courageous. Even while I have trembled with fear and doubt, I have shown up. I have willingly dived right in, meeting my shadows and getting to know them. No matter how hard, I have looked straight into the fear and never gave up processing. I have embodied the wisdom that "the only way out is through." I am grateful for my commitment to the true meaning of self-care. I thought self-care was pampering, but in reality, self-care is sometimes sitting in whatever anxiety and fear comes up and *not avoiding it*.

I can't thank myself enough for the amount of therapy and healing I have done. I started therapy when I was 20 years old. I didn't know anyone personally that was in therapy, but I went for it. I went to my college student center and asked if they knew of any resources for long-term therapy. They gave me a few recommendations, and I went with one of them. I am grateful for my curiosity for wanting to try therapy, and for my ability to prioritize the importance of my mental and emotional health. I am thankful for my 20 year old self every day for making that brave decision to go to therapy, and I can never thank her enough.

INFINITE GRATITUDE

Just like how I can't thank everyone and myself enough, nobody can thank me enough. My mom can't thank me enough for the amount of healing I did to repair our relationship. My dad can't thank me enough for all the times I validated his pain. My sister can't thank me enough for being her partner in every emotional and physical family event.

Because everyone can't thank me enough, I can't thank everyone and myself enough. We should all stop trying to seek validation in others. If we stopped putting pressure on others to soothe our anxieties and stopped outsourcing our job of validating ourselves, our world would be a kinder place.

We often talk about intergenerational and ancestral trauma in the context of pain that we have received. The river flows and doesn't choose what runs with it. It just does. As much as I have gotten trauma, I have also received ancestral gifts. When I listen to stories of my great-aunts, grandparents, and great-grandparents, I see that they are all alive in me. Their qi (chi) is flowing through me, and I can never honor them enough.

I can never thank my mom, dad, sister, family, teachers, guides, ancestors, friends, and myself enough. My sister and I come from a strong lineage of badass women, and I can never thank my ancestors enough. I can never give enough thanks to Source and all the gifts I have been given. If I were to attempt to say all the ways I am grateful, I would die before I was finished. This book would also never be done. My appreciation will never be fully captured, but I hope that the ways

I love infinitely will leave an imprint of my gratitude. Gratitude is the key to having a meaningful life.

> "If the only prayer you ever say in your entire life is 'Thank you,' it will be enough."
>
> — Meister Eckhart

> "In the end, though, maybe we must all give up trying to pay back the people in this world who sustain our lives. In the end, maybe it's wiser to surrender before the miraculous scope of human generosity and to just keep saying thank you, forever and sincerely, for as long as we have voices."
>
> — Elizabeth Gilbert

3.9

SHADOW OF SERVICE: MANIPULATING AND TAKING ADVANTAGE OF OTHERS

ENVY BRINGS CLARITY

In one of our energy-fueled writing sessions, I started having this icky prickly feeling in the pit of my stomach, and the sensation would quickly spread to the back of my throat. It was *envy*. I was envious of Winnie's ability to write with gusto and have every thought, word, and lesson organized in a clear flow. I was struggling with organizing my stories and stumbling through writer's block. I would look across at Winnie with awe as she oozed it all out. The book was coming out of her pores, and I was amazed. And *extremely* envious.

In the beginning of the writing process, we both said that Source was using us as vessels to write. Seeing Winnie type fast with a piercing focus made me feel as if my connection with Source wasn't as powerful as hers. She was a full witch, and I was just this awkward pubescent teenage witch trying to keep up.

Quickly, I was on my shame elevator, going deeper and deeper down into the levels of how could you's and what is wrong with you's. How could I be such trash and be envious of someone generous and loving and kind like Winnie? *What on earth was wrong with me?*

Then something occurred to me. What if I told Winnie what I was experiencing? Normally, if I feel the envy monster creeping up, I pummel the monster deep with shame, guilt, self-hatred, and disgust. Eventually leading to an emotionally constipated self hiding in the corner, and avoiding the person or situation that brought out the envy in the first place. While Winnie was fiercely writing, I admitted, "I am having a very weird experience right now." She dropped everything and instructed me to tell her everything that was going on. I sheepishly told her I was feeling a lot of shame and didn't know how to say it out loud. She laughed and asked how much worse it could be than her dirtiest shameful trash she laid out for me to see. My first thought was *true*. But then my second thought was *this was different* because I was feeling this about her.

However, *because* Winnie shared her deepest darkest shameful feelings, I felt safe to tell her about the envy I was feeling towards her. I felt safe because I love Winnie and all that she is—not in spite of her shame, but *because of all* of it. I love her for sharing with me her divine goddess healer self *and* her humanness. As soon as I told her about my envy, I was relieved but scared. It was risky to tell someone I am so grateful for that I was also jealous.

A powerful healing occurred. Winnie did not judge me or move away from me. She *empowered* me. She told me that envy was a way of getting clarity on what I desired and wanted. The reason why I was envious was that I desired to be how powerful Winnie was. My envy was showing me how I wanted to serve others. By recognizing the power I already have and using it to be the best healer I can be, I get to step into my unique expression of the Tao. Winnie is her own unique expression of the Tao, and I am my own. Instead of looking at Winnie and trying to emulate her power, I get to adjust and use my energy in connecting with my power.

It is truly healing to have an envious feeling that usually goes straight to shame instead bring clarity. I am grateful for my ability to sit in the discomfort of telling Winnie the truth because so many layers of healing have come from it. I am grateful to Winnie for holding space for me and empowering me. We show up for others by showing up for ourselves. By telling Winnie my shame, I also show up for myself in releasing my shame. By Winnie loving me through my shame, she also loves herself through her shame. What a beautiful way to bond in our sisterhood and a beautiful lesson on how I get to serve others that also feel shame.

I also know that I am only 29 years old. I have been blossoming and maturing, but I am just beginning. I have experienced exponential growth up to this moment, but I also still have the rest of my life and more adventures to encounter and learn from.

The next time I feel envy, I now know it is an opportunity to gain clarity for what I truly desire. Envy nudges us closer to what is calling out to us. It shows us how we can better serve others. I get closer to my own unique expression of the Tao by gaining clarity with every feeling I observe and dive into.

EVERY SINGLE MODALITY MATTERS

I am a healing slut. I am open to healing in all ways that work, and I am not loyal to only one type of healing. I love à la carte style for everything: eating, healing, and beliefs. I pick and choose from different healing practices and modalities and keep what I resonate most with. I am a spiritual seeker, and I believe in following my curiosity. That means I believe in the power of psychotherapy, Traditional Chinese Medicine, acupuncture, reiki energy healing, tarot readings, akashic records readings, shamanic journeying, sound baths, yoga, art, music, creativity, and more.

It is wild to see different modalities peacocking, showing off with superiority trying to prove one is better than the other. Some medical doctors scoff at psychologists and don't respect them on the same level of being a doctor. In contrast, some psychologists feel superior to therapists because they got their doctorate. Some LMFTs (Licensed Marriage and Family therapists) feel more emotionally equipped than LCSWs (Licensed Clinical Social Workers), and then the judgment reverses. This happens in acupuncture and energy healing as well. Every modality thinks they are the best.

However, *every single modality matters*. One is not better or worse than the other, and trying to create hierarchy in modalities is a waste of energy. Don't we all have the same purpose of being here to serve humanity? If we all respected one another for each individual's unique gifts, we could all join together with the intention to help serve in raising human consciousness.

TURNING MY TRAUMAS INTO SERVICE

> "I consider the world, this Earth, to be like a school, and our life the classrooms."
>
> — Oprah Winfrey

One of the gifts of trauma is that I was able to see how all the times I hurt others were trauma responses. I took advantage of others' kindness, and it was because I was trying to protect myself, while in reality, I was perpetuating my hurt. Having compassion for my wounded self has taught me to have compassion for others that are wounded.

If it weren't for my hardest lessons and my most sensitive wounds, I would not have awakened to my soul's purpose of serving others. I get to take my trauma and all of my lemons, turn it into lemonade and share the sweetness with all around me. The deep hurt I have endured in my life makes me a better therapist and healer. I get to have a profound understanding and compassion for my clients' pain because of what I have gone through. I have been given the opportunities and gifts of resiliency, love, and service.

I believe that we are all spiritual beings and souls that have specific reasons for being human in this lifetime. I ask myself and Source, why is it that in this lifetime, I am human? Why is it that I happen to be a Korean American woman who is a daughter of immigrants that experienced the traumas in my life? What are the lessons I am to learn in this lifetime?

> "Why are you here? That's the ultimate question that you get to answer with every action, thought, and feeling. There is a calling on your life. What will be your answer?"
>
> — Oprah Winfrey

I don't know all the answers, and I never will. I don't need to. I do know that I needed to experience the full scope of being human: feeling joy, love, shame, disgust, hate, anger, and more. I needed to learn how to have compassion for myself and others. Maybe I am Korean American because I get to learn how to live in two worlds at once, being Korean and being American. Maybe it's so that I get to learn the respect for a collectivistic culture as the admiration pumps through my veins. Maybe I needed to be a woman to learn how to be empowered in a patriarchal society. Maybe I am here to have strong roots in my human lineage of ancestors. Maybe I get to not just serve humanity, but serve my ancestors and help process the traumas that they couldn't process in their lifetimes.

"There is not one experience, no matter how devastating, no matter how torturous it may appear to have been, there is nothing that's ever wasted. Everything that is happening to you is being drawn into your life as a means to help you evolve into who you were really meant to be here on Earth. It's not the thing that matters, it's what that thing opens within you."

— Oprah Winfrey

3.10

SHADOW OF ENLIGHTENMENT: SHAME, NOT KNOWING AND AVOIDING OUR DIVINITY, RESISTANT TO THE GOD/SOURCE/UNIVERSE PLAN

LOSING MY CONNECTION WITH GOD

Growing up in a Christian household, I learned about God, heaven, hell, sinning, shame, and being "saved." As I got older, I rejected God fiercely. Even the word God was triggering, and I would avoid anything that had an ounce of religion or the word Jesus or God. Whenever my mom would talk about her relationship with God, I would shut down and either tell her I didn't want to talk about God or start to space out. I was a big No on God until my mid-twenties.

I also had beef with God because God didn't answer my desperate prayers to bring my mom back. I also hated God because my mom would use God as a reason why she couldn't leave my stepdad yet or that the timing didn't feel right for certain areas of her life. I would be furious towards God for keeping my mom asleep in a daze of escapism and avoidance. I rejected God fiercely and would even judge others for believing in God.

Then something happened. I started opening myself to the possibility of God during my healing journey. It was not God, the being, but rather an energy or a warmth. I would start to see the beauty in nature and feel a blossoming of a deep connection with a Higher Power. I remember going to the Natural History Museum and crying when I looked into a beautiful geode, feeling the presence of Earth. I would tear up at the magnificence of a tree and the perfect sacred geometry in a flower. I still would get triggered by the word "God" but I started to awaken to realizing that I was rejecting a doctrine and not God.

THE STORY OF MY ABORTION

I had an abortion with my partner Eric in the summer of 2019. We were one of the lucky ones. We found out about the pregnancy early on, we happened to live in a progressive state, there was no problem getting an appointment since this was before the pandemic, and I wasn't alone. Eric was with me every step of the way. Although I wasn't alone, it was an incredibly lonely experience.

It's funny because naively, I was nonchalant about getting an abortion. As soon as we found out we were pregnant, I was just like, alrighty an abortion it is! I had no qualms about getting one. The people at Planned Parenthood were incredibly kind and loving. I was lucky to be able to choose between the pill and the procedure. I took one pill at the clinic and followed directions for the subsequent pills when I got home. I didn't have any emotional attachment or anything to having the abortion—at first.

But let me tell you how my abortion humbled me and knocked me *the hell down* to my knees.

I bled so much after the abortion, which was to be expected. However, I did not stop bleeding for almost three long years. Every time I sat down on the toilet to pee, I was constantly reminded that my body was no longer my own. Eventually, I would feel betrayed by my own body and quickly become disconnected from my fleshy home. I soon became numb to protect myself from the physical and emotional pain of feeling trapped in my own being. I felt like a prisoner stuck in my broken body.

The numbness came to me quietly. Just like depression, I didn't know how numb I was until I was already so deep in my numbness. Numbness gave me the illusion of escapism and protected me from feeling unbearable pain, but it also dampened my joy, my desires, my magic, and my intuition. It also cut me off from accessing my divine femininity and my sexuality. Sure I didn't feel agonizing pain, but I also didn't crave, want, and desire the joys of life. I was rarely hungry for food, love, intimacy, and touch.

The insidious nature of numbness is that because I was no longer in active pain, I thought I was "finished" processing the abortion. I wasn't full-on raging, and it was a year past the abortion, so I thought I was over it. I talked about it incessantly in therapy, and I unconsciously lied to myself to believe that I was done processing because I *so badly wanted* to be done. I was in full-on denial because that is how out of touch I was with my body.

I ignored the brewing resentment I felt and all the warning signs that my rage was going to soon explode. I blamed my rage on the pandemic and the loneliness of the lockdowns. I blamed my rage on the injustices of our society as we all felt the horror of the murder of George Floyd and the killing of Breonna Taylor. I blamed it on the inequality of wealth as people were getting evicted at the height of the pandemic. I blamed it on the upcoming elections and how voter suppression was still rampant. I blamed it on the deep division in our country. I blamed it on the racism against Asian people and how Asian elders were being attacked on the streets in broad daylight. I was full on raging, but I still was not looking at my abortion. 2020 became the perfect rage cocktail storm for me as the world was falling apart, and I was also deteriorating with it.

Although I was numb, a God moment occurred. I felt an urge with a little wink from the Divine that I should change my dissertation topic to abortion stigma. I was previously going to research art therapy on intergenerational trauma on Korean Americans. Most professors of mine have warned me and every cohort not to choose a dissertation topic that is too personal. But I knew very deep in my gut, thanks to Divine Intervention, that I needed to choose the *most* personal. It was like I knew but also didn't know. By choosing to research and look into abortion stigma, I knew I was going to step on all the landmines, face all the crap I was avoiding, and look deep at my pain. I also knew this was going to be the push I needed to launch myself out of numbness. I felt like my dissertation was going to be a gift to myself as a courageous act of self-love to willingly dive into the pit of hellfire. I also felt it would be a gift to the field of psychology because abortion stigma research was limiting and lacking.

As I was writing my dissertation in early 2021 and facing some of my deepest pains, I was flailing helplessly into deep despair. I lost my appetite, my never-ending period blood was never a fresh pigment of red, I had horrible eczema flare-ups, my skin was so dry no matter how much I moisturized, and I felt a level of fatigue and exhaustion that I had never experienced before. There would be days where I would sleep 16 hours straight and still wake up drained. One time, I slept 36 hours straight without waking up to eat, sleep, or drink water. My body was shutting down. My relationship with Eric was on the rocks. I was physically, mentally, emotionally, energetically, and spiritually exhausted. I was tired of everything, but most of all, I was tired *of being tired*. I was so sick of myself.

I was barely functioning, and one day, Eric told me he was feeling very disconnected from me. He was questioning whether I even still liked him and if I was checked out of the relationship. The truth was that I was checked out of *everything*. I felt completely alone in my pain, and even though he was being supportive, he didn't know what it was like to be bleeding nonstop for years. I didn't want the relationship to end since my love for Eric never stopped, but I also was entirely exhausted. I was avoiding Eric because I was growing very angry and resentful towards him while writing my dissertation, and I didn't want to lash out at him. I lost my ability to be present with him, myself, and everyone else.

Eric felt as if I was not giving into our relationship anymore. However, I felt like I was giving everything I had. I was giving into the relationship by going through all the pain from the abortion. I was holding all the daily reminders of the physical and emotional pain for the both of us. I felt like I was doing the heavy lifting, and how dare he question whether I was giving in to the relationship. I was giving *everything* I had. It's just that I had nothing left to give because I was barely surviving.

Eric and I went on a trip to Big Bear in May of 2021, almost two years after the abortion. It was to hopefully repair some of our relationship and also celebrate the end of our semester, my successful dissertation proposal, and to spend some quality time together. On this trip, we were both not doing well. The elevation made Eric completely restless while I was so deep in my depression and pain that I barely wanted to even go outside of our cabin. One night, I took a huge amount of magic mushrooms and sobbed for over 24 hours straight. I finally was letting myself *fully* feel all my pain. I felt fragile, raw, and highly sensitive. I surrendered and stopped resisting the deep hurt I was feeling. I was finally and thankfully no longer stuck in my numbness. I could feel every single open wound, and I was in agonizing pain.

I wanted to start healing, but I was still experiencing extreme fatigue and exhaustion. My body was still shut down even though I was no longer emotionally numb. I went to my general practitioner and got blood work done. I wasn't iron deficient or lacking in vital nutrients. Medically, I was okay, but I did not *feel* okay. I felt like I was slowly dying.

Then I started seeing both Winnie and Christina for acupuncture and reiki energy healing in July of 2021, exactly two years after the abortion and shortly after the Big Bear trip. Winnie and Christina both changed my life in a radical way. Seeing both of them consistently on a weekly or every other week basis opened healing doors for me that I never knew existed. Going to them not only was healing me personally, but it was teaching me to become a better healer as a talk therapist. At first, I couldn't physically feel the Qi (Chi) flowing through me, but I would leave every session feeling better and stronger. Each session would bring me closer to reconnecting with my body. I would start to become more aware of my body and recognize my heart beating fast, the coldness of my feet, the small blockage in my left hip, and the discomfort in my right leg. I would attend Winnie's weekly Healing Circles, happily take the herbs Christina recommended, and feel my heart open as I settled more into my body. Trust in Divine Timing because if it weren't for the six to seven years of talk therapy I did with M, I wouldn't have been able to be fully open to accepting and taking in all the healing wisdom.

After a few months of consistent sessions with Winnie and Christina, I finally had more strength to look another level deeper into my abortion. The abortion led me to look at a cumulative mountain of my pain. I was staring into the abyss of my fear, doubts, shame, resistance, codependency, anger, resentment, disgust, limiting beliefs, rage, judgments, avoidance, expectations, confusion, an attachment to my pain, and the need to blame.

I started to see how I was resistant to letting Eric into my heart and how I was blaming him for all my pain. I was lashing out at him because I was the one to carry all the physical consequences of the abortion. It was *me* who was the one bleeding nonstop. It was *me* who was the one that got the IUD painfully inserted into my uterus so that we could prevent another pregnancy. It was *me* who had to go to all the gynecology appointments. It was *me* who was exhausted, depleted, tired, and so wiped out. It was *me* who was a woman and suffered under the patriarchy. ME ME ME.

But, it was also *me* who took my body for granted, and it took a crisis like the abortion to wake me up. It was *me* who was shutting Eric out and not letting him help me. It was *me* who was resistant to surrendering. It was *me* not being compassionate to myself. It was *me* who was staying stuck in my shame cycle. I saw how Eric was suffering under the patriarchy too. I saw how powerless he felt as he couldn't share the physical burden of the pain with me. I saw how he accepted with loving understanding all of my unfair blame and resentment that I threw at him. He didn't reject me or fight back once. All he did was ask me to let him in. I was blaming him for the patriarchy and for not taking my pain away when neither of those was his responsibility. And even if he did want to take responsibility, it is impossible for him to take my pain away and lift the weight of the patriarchy off of me.

Only I can heal my pain. Only I can heal my wounds.

Only I can fully understand my pain. Even though Winnie had an abortion too and can have incredible compassion for me, only I can completely see and validate the entirety of my pain.

I realized I was trying to show Eric my pain so that he could fully understand me, which is an unattainable ask and would leave me even more resentful. I learned that you diminish your healing when you try to "perform" your pain in the way that another person understands it and sees you. *Nobody* will see you the way you can see yourself.

Another huge lesson I learned was that our mind holds onto pain because it is the ultimate defeating card to play in order to manipulate others' behaviors. For example, if I said to Eric, "Wow. I had an incredible day. I had such a pep in my step all day! Can you take out the trash?" versus "Ughhhhh, I had such a hard day and my stomach hurts. Can you take out the trash?" What scenario will more likely get Eric to take out the trash? The answer is the one where I am complaining about my day.

Our mind holds onto our pain and does not let go easily because why would we ever give up a checkmate move? Our attachment to pain gives us the ability to manipulate others, but it also keeps us stuck in victimhood. We have to *own* our part in the co-creation of our own suffering. We may not have started the pain, but we have a part in staying *attached* to our pain. Nobody can heal your pain but you.

As I am writing this book, my periods have still not returned to what they were before the abortion. Since seeing Winnie and Christina, I have experienced small pauses of not bleeding even though I have also experienced weeks of steady bleeding. Yet, I no longer feel disgust or shame when I see the blood every time I go pee. I trust the process and my healing journey as it continually evolves.

I am so thankful for my abortion experience. It brought me to my knees and was my ticket to waking the hell up. I am so grateful I took the opportunity to open my eyes and face what I was resisting. I have had many blessings from the pain of my abortion. I get to have a sisterhood with Winnie. I get to have a badass dissertation on abortion stigma. I get to have a stronger intimate relationship with Eric. I get to be a healer for others going through deep pain. I get to be connected to my body and actually feel all the blockages melting in every healing session I have with Winnie or Christina. I get to be attuned with myself and others. I get to experience the fullness of my joy. I get to bask in the warmth of my growth. I get to enjoy the journey towards freedom. I had an *awakening through crisis,* and this is how I know for sure that EVERYTHING IS A GIFT.

"There is one irrefutable law of the universe: We are each responsible for our own life. If you're holding anyone else accountable for your happiness, you're wasting your time. You must be fearless enough to give yourself the love you didn't receive."

— Oprah Winfrey

SORRY NOT SORRY

M fairly warned me that once you step on the spiritual path, you can't turn around. You can't *undo* the awakening. When I first started seeing M in 2015, I was not on the spiritual path, but after a few years of working together, I started opening myself up to the possibility of a Higher Power. That was when I would have my experiences with nature and Earth. Because this was around the same time that I discovered my pain under my anger, I felt so raw and fragile. My sensitive self was the one that stepped on the spiritual path, and there would be times where I would beg if I could just turn back around, that it was too hard. But I knew I couldn't. Deep down, I knew that I also wouldn't want to. I was blind for so long, and although awakening can first be blinding and harsh, I was seeing so clearly for the first time. I was on the path, and there was no getting off of it.

Life can be treacherous and complicated, but the journey of self-discovery and connection with the Divine is unequivocally worthwhile. It is an act of courage to take the brave step onto the spiritual path because there is no turning back. However, each step will bring one closer to oneself and others and show how we are all more connected than we can comprehend.

"Wherever you are in your journey, I hope you, too, will keep encountering challenges. It is a blessing to be able to survive them, to be able to keep putting one foot in front of the other — to be in a position to make the climb up life's mountain, knowing that the summit still lies ahead. And every experience is a valuable teacher."

— Oprah Winfrey

RECONNECTING WITH GOD

It was only until very recently, in 2021, that I finally embraced the word God. Previously, I would say Soul or Higher Power or the Divine. Now, I was able to say and use the word God and not feel the need to prepare for a negative impact. When I say God, it is another word for Source, Spirit, Soul, All, Higher Power, the Divine, and the One. To me, God is not just a being. God is love, and God exists in everything and everyone. There is God in me. There is God in you. There is God in the trees, the air, the sun, the infinite space in our universe, and the space between you and me. My definition of God may not align with another's definition of God, but this is also how I stay open to others' connections with their God.

Because there is God/Source in all things and beings, when you love someone, you are loving yourself too. Because God is in me, when I spew hate towards others, I am hating the God in them, which in turn is also me. So when you hate someone, you are rejecting God and yourself too. As human beings, we are not going to always be able to love everyone and everything. But if we can try to take *all* of life's opportunities to choose love, not just to each other but *especially* ourselves, we can hold each others' hands as each individual heals.

"What God intended for you goes far beyond anything you can imagine."

— Oprah Winfrey

PART IV

THE TREASURES OF SHADOW WORK

4.1

WINNIE'S GIFTS FROM SHADOW WORK

The Law of Yin Yang says, "All things are made of Yin and Yang." Water is not less than fire; moon is not less than sun, feminine is not less than masculine, and shadow is not less than light.

Shadow work isn't to say that shadow is bad, and we need to let it go. Shadow work isn't about getting rid of the shadow but bringing ourselves back to balance and flow. Our spiritual journey isn't to go to the light but to remove the struggle and flow with the Tao. *Dwelling or preferring the light can lead to suffering.*

Shadow work is understanding the deep Tao wisdom—yin needs yang, yang needs yin. There is yin within yang, yang within yin. Yin is constantly transforming into yang, and yang is constantly transforming into yin.

Shadow transforms to light like night is followed by day. Light transforms to shadow like day is followed by night. We cannot only have day and skip the night.

The key to Oneness is to stay in balance. When we are giving others love and light, we need to make sure to stay rooted in our shadow (be "selfish" and give to ourselves before giving to others). When we are in the dark, stay guided by our light (be "divine" and surrender our pain and let others help us).

EVERYONE AND EVERYTHING THAT HAPPENS IS A PERFECT GIFT FROM THE TAO

My teachers saved my life, my parents gave me life, John supported my life, my kids motivated and drove the progress in my life.

We all do what we have to do. Instead of assuming the worst of others and being defensive about how others will take advantage of us, can we trust that we are all doing our best, getting things done, being resourceful, weaving connections, and making the best of what we got?

The people I love most gave me the greatest pain and also the greatest pleasure. I also gave them the greatest pain and greatest pleasure. We signed up for this human body to experience pain and pleasure. Remember Shinzen Young's four equations we discussed at the beginning of the book:

1. Pain x resistance = suffering

2. Pain x equanimity = purification

3. Pleasure x dwelling = frustration

4. Pleasure x equanimity = fulfillment

Every person is divine. Every person is a gift. Enlightenment is accepting the reality of the present moment and then releasing it—whether it is pain or pleasure, we do not dwell.

All the pain and pleasure serves our enlightenment. If we surrender control, we will be able to be present and dance with the pain and pleasure that shows up in our life. The goal of the spiritual journey is to give up struggles and dance with the Tao.

"Feel your feelings, face your shadows, stay in the NOW." — Mei Ling Tsui

Intuitive medium @Meiling.intuitive

Hate is part of the human experience. We need to experience and unwrap hate to learn to deepen our love. Being connected is a core human need. Can we loosen our attachment to being right and find more compassion for ourselves and others?

When jealousy and stress show up, we honor it. Embrace it. Just like envy can show us where we long to step into our greatest service, stress shows us how deeply we care about a cause. Triggers show us how deeply we care about a person—the more intense the trigger, the more deeply we care! Instead of resisting the jealousy or stress when they show up, just breathe compassion, bring in the wisdom to loosen the attachments to the story, and redirect that energy into service! Language is a powerful tool. Language helps us set our intention. Language can help us gain clarity. But language can also keep us locked and trapped in our suffering. Be present with how we talk to ourselves. Be present with the dialogue that shapes our reactions.

Stress and jealousy are just an energy that is yang. Yang qi rises, yin qi descends. When jealousy and stress show up, make use of the yang energy to get work done! Adrenaline makes us run faster and break our personal records. We need yang to break through.

The reason we have a negative association with stress is that under the patriarchy, we value work over rest. We value analysis, structure, rules, discipline, overgoing with the flow, creativity, fun, and accepting what is. If we valued yin and yang equally, if we valued masculine and feminine equally, we would appreciate when the adrenaline is pumping in our blood and all the great things we can achieve under stress. When we integrate yin and yang, there can be work in play and play in work! We can work at the beach, or we can eat fun snacks while we work.

THE PAST DOES NOT DEFINE OUR FUTURE

The past does not define our future. We have infinite potential. The past determines where we stand right now, but the past does not dictate our choices going forward.

The gift of doing the shadow work is that each time I work through a shadow, I purify, and my light shines brighter. The shadow work helps me know and trust myself. I enjoy my spiritual channels so much! I enjoy receiving all the abundance in love, support, and protection from the spiritual realm. For example, just today, as I caught a glimpse of my co-parent's eyes, my guides told me, "You knew he was trouble, and you ignored all the red flags." I laughed, because of course, the version of John that I met when I was 22 was 無情 (His heart was closed). After three weeks of dating, he told me that he either wanted to date a girl for sex or marriage, and I didn't fall into either category. I should have known that these are glaring signs of an emotionally unavailable man who has not healed his childhood wounds. I should have seen the red flags.

I take responsibility! My vibrational field contained negative karmic information that would attract a person who would make me feel like a woman's body is a man's property, that is either used for sex or controlled in a cage. To be fair to John, he has done so much therapy, and he has gained so much empathy and compassion over the 19 years we were together, and I am honestly impressed by his growth. Since he won't thank me for my contribution, I will go ahead and give myself the credit—John cannot be the man he is today without my love. All these years, I poured my love into this man. Yes, with the anal-retentive streak of a straight-A student, I tried to be the perfect wife and the perfect mom. Yes, I am going to say "You're welcome" to all his future girlfriends, thanking me for opening the Tin Man.

On the reverse token, he should have also seen all the red flags about me. I cried and used my tears as manipulation and begged him to date me one more week. "Let's hang out for one more week? We can eat Chinese takeout on the couch? Please allow me to hang out with you. There is no obligation, no risk, and no commitment." Oh my God, if anyone ever comes across as a complete powerless begging victim with no self-respect and complete worthlessness, RUN! Of course, she would turn out to be suicidal and need a lot of therapy before she could be in a healthy conscious relationship!

Or perhaps, we can see the perfection, that everything happened exactly the way it happened. John was the perfect guy for my spiritual journey, and I was the perfect girl for his growth. Thank you, John, with the greatest gratitude, for delivering my awakening in this lifetime! I needed him for a crisis to awaken, and *oh yes*, did I make lemonade out of the lemons!

I was John's victim, perpetrator, and rescuer. John was also my victim, perpetrator, and rescuer. Whether he can see himself as my perpetrator and see me as his rescuer is his business. Let the past be in the past. I don't need his apology, and I don't need his appreciation. I pray that one day he will open his heart to me because how he opens his heart to me is how he opens his heart to himself.

For months after the divorce, I requested to have movie night or Sunday brunch as a family with John and the kids. I wanted to let the kids feel that their parents are one team, one family under two roofs. John kept his boundaries with me. While I respect that, honestly, he should be the one requesting to have a friendship with me. He should be the one that is requesting my presence over a cup of tea or unlimited free healing sessions from me. Why? If we look at our relationship as a transaction or energy exchange, it is because of the financial stability that he provided that I was able to get my medical degree and spiritual training, open a private healing practice right after graduation, and semi-retire my healing practice to become a teacher and author. If I am any kind of successful, it is because of the supporting foundation that he provided and continues to provide for the rest of my life. If he doesn't choose to receive my love, he is a victim and a perpetrator of his own boundaries, pride, and fears! He is the one that is robbing himself of the abundance of love and healing that he has already paid for!

All the rejections I felt from John are empty! When I step out of my attachment to victimhood, I can see the emptiness of my suffering. Everyone who has ever said "No" to me is because they are not ready for me, *and* I am not ready for them. Keep believing in Oneness, keep melting, keep softening. Be the first to delete the limiting beliefs. Be the first to open our hearts. Spiritual practice is about courage and knowing our infinity!

GIFT OF TRAUMA

My dad is now my biggest fan and supporter. Of all the believers of my healing abilities, I am most grateful for my dad's willingness to trust me.

My dad has been one of the most respected surgeons in Hong Kong, practicing Western medicine for 54 years. Western medicine practitioners use evidence-based medicine, prescribe pills, and perform surgeries. My dad trusts me completely with my Traditional Chinese Medicine practice and my spiritual healing practice. One time he told me he had a painful rash on the phone, and I asked for his permission to "give me a chance to work on him." By the end of the call, the rash and the pain were gone. He told me, "You are simply marvelous. This is some form of therapy and healing beyond explanations or imagination to our Western medicine culture. How did I gain this ability?"

It is in our darkest, most hopeless, and desperate moments that we know God. The gift of trauma is that we learn to surrender and use the power of prayer for divine intervention. Trauma helps us cultivate compassion for our suffering and be empathetic to others. In my darkest moments, I got really good at praying and asking for help. That's basically what I do when others give me a chance to work on them. I guide them into prayers. How much healing happens depends on how much they are willing to receive the unconditional love of God.

Trauma also helps us connect. Every time we share our story, not only do we enjoy the compassion and validation from others, but we also help others feel less alone in their suffering. Therefore, when we share our pain, we serve others as we also serve ourselves.

I used to walk around with oceans of shame about what happened in the past. How can anyone respect me after they find out about all my mistakes? But it is precisely my courage and strength in standing in my authenticity that earns the trust. It is in the vulnerability and my humanness that connects others to me. Sharing my darkness gives others permission to love all parts of them, including their darkness.

During the divorce, there were countless dark nights of the soul. Instead of cycling between the four classic trauma responses of fight, flight, fawn, and freeze, I learned how to graduate from my trauma. Here's the thing. Nobody can ever undo a rape. Nobody can ever undo verbal abuse. Nobody can ever undo sending their child to a foreign country. I cannot take back anything I have said or done to John or my kids. Trauma cannot be "erased". If you lost a leg in the war, you aren't getting your old leg back. However, *peace* can be found in the *center of the storm*.

There exists a part of us, our original soul, which cannot be broken and cannot be traumatized. This part of us that is eternal and does not die. In Christianity, we call this "Christ consciousness". In Reiki, we call this "Buddha nature". In yoga, we call this "the light in me". Everyone has Christ consciousness, Buddha nature, the light, or whatever you want to call it in your spiritual tradition. While we cannot erase the trauma, we *can control* our response. We get there by integrating our darkness with our light. In Buddhism, we call this practice "Inviting Mara to tea", allowing the Buddha nature within us to sit down and have tea with the demon within us. In Radiant Heart meditation, we call this "inviting our pain into our heart or breathing compassion into the part of us that feels pain." Our heart is infinitely spacious and can love/hug any challenges that arise.

"YOU are what you can control."

-Katie Davie @coparentingPeacefully

What is the true meaning that God is everywhere? That means God is in you, God is in me, and God is in the very air we breathe. Therefore, we can surrender all of our pain and suffering to our hearts, others' hearts, and also to the sun, moon, ocean, trees, earth, and animals.

Every day I continue to open my heart to the God in me, the God in you, and the God in all. I hope you are inspired to do the same.

EVERYONE IS OUR MIRROR

Remember that everyone is our mirror. How we trust ourselves is how we trust others. I want to receive myself totally, so I can receive you totally. How someone shows up for us is how they show up for themselves. Next time instead of getting mad at someone, can we find compassion for how we feel but also how badly they must also feel inside?

Every time we are triggered, we know that that is a "report card" that there is stickiness or resistance in our mind. Instead of "I am ashamed of my darkness," can we shift into "I am afraid to open up to my light?" Can we surrender control, trust that the universe is helping us expand into our soul purpose, and all the help will show up in diving timing?

> "Open up and stop being afraid of yourself."
>
> @PhilGoodLife

Perhaps we can reframe.

Victim => Lover (receiving from others)

Rescuer => Supporter (providing and uplifting)

Perpetrator => Protector (slaying, breaking, penetrating, and cutting through our illusions)

Master Rulin Xiu teaches a mantra in her *Divine Love*[1] book and course: "We are infinitely loved, protected and supported, by the whole cosmos, divine Tao and source, beyond our wildest dreams."

Whenever someone gives us pain, they are really giving us an opportunity to come home to our hearts.

THE GIFT OF DENIAL = BE GENTLE WITH OURSELVES

Shadow work can be hard and overwhelming. Sometimes what we need is not to dig but to rest. Sometimes we don't have the bandwidth to process our traumas. Sometimes what we need is to put a Band-Aid on it instead of opening the wound to get the poison out. Sometimes what we need is to bring comfort to the victim.

Yes, there is a gift in denial, in avoiding, lying, escaping, and numbing the pain. Sometimes the regret is too intense. Sometimes doing the shadow work and being really honest about what we've done would make us hate ourselves too much. Sometimes the grief of losing our loved ones is unbearable, and we are not functional. Sometimes what we need is to take the medications and get some rest.

Can we bring compassion to ourselves when all we want to do is drink a magical potion that will make us forget about our pains?

Can we bring compassion to ourselves for wanting to avoid feeling the difficult emotions?

It is okay to give ourselves a break. It is okay to recognize that life is too overwhelming. It is okay to take a break from processing or healing our traumas. It is okay to take medications that lessen the intensity of the emotions.

It is okay not to want to sit with the pain. It is okay to want to get away from it all.

Find patience and forgive ourselves for all the times we were tired of the process and didn't want to do the work. "Dear the parts of me that want to avoid, deny, numb, escape: I love you no matter what you've done in the past, I love you no matter what you choose right now. I give you permission to run away from your feelings. I trust that after you take a break to find some space, you will bounce back stronger. I love you. I hold you in my arms."

THE DOWNSIDE OF PROCRASTINATING SHADOW WORK

There is a price to pay when we ignore our shadow. This literally happened to me today. Someone made mistakes, and I got really upset by "their incompetence." (I know!). Anyway, I tried to spiritually bypass myself. "Just let that go. Don't let that bother you." See, that didn't work. Because the rest of the day, the universe kept serving me incompetence after incompetence. When I procrastinated on processing the frustration, I started experiencing the world through the lens of frustration, and I manifested more frustration into my life! (Aaagggh!)

Therefore, whenever we find ourselves in a messy situation, it really pays to stop blaming everything on everyone else. Journey inside and ask for spiritual help to gain clarity.

My guides showed me: "Competence is good enough. Incompetence is not good enough. The reason I am triggered by another's incompetence is that I haven't forgiven myself for the mistakes I have made! I am still judging and punishing myself for my bad performance in the past. The greatest lesson isn't to forgive others or stop judging others for their mistakes. The greatest lesson is to forgive *me*, to open my heart so that divine love can flow from my heart. Can you rise above the mud like the lotus?"

Doing shadow work truly helps us drop the resistance and enjoy the perfection of God's creation and God's plan.

CONFESSION FROM A HYPOCRITE

You know I'm a hypocrite, right? I want you to read my book, but I don't really like to read. I want to be on TV shows, but I don't watch TV. I want a lot of followers, but if you are reading my books or watching my videos, then you are watching me play from the bleachers instead of playing your own game in the arena! While I bring compassion to my inner hypocrite and love my ego tenderly, don't take me too seriously. Don't take yourself too seriously. In Tao Te Ching chapter 38:

The Master does nothing,

yet he leaves *nothing* undone.

The **ordinary** man is *always doing* things,

yet many more are left to be done.

The **kind** man does something,

yet *something* remains undone.

The **just** man does something,

and leaves *many things* to be done.

The **moral** man does something,

and when no one responds,

he rolls up his sleeves and uses force.

I used to be attached to being *kind, just,* and *moral,* and I was always doing something, always unable to finish everything, and I get frustrated when others don't do what they are supposed to do. Loosen the attachment to getting things right. Loosen the attachment to success. It is in surrendering (aka not controlling every detail) that we achieve "doing, not doing."

TRUSTING THE TAO IN YOURSELF

My goal is to help you trust yourself, trust the Tao within you, give yourself permission to come into the fullest expression of your soul purpose.

I am so blessed to have Raven, Master Sha, and Dr. Chu as my teachers because each of them is an example of coming into their own expression of the Tao.

- Raven leveraged all of her psychology, Tibetan Buddhism, and shamanic teachers to birth her own Integrated Shakti Reiki and became a beacon of the Divine Feminine. (www.integrativewisdompath.com)

- Master Sha leveraged his Taoist TCM teacher and his calligraphy teacher to create Tao healing Calligraphy and spread love, peace, and harmony in the world. (www.drsha.com)

- Dr. Chu dedicated his whole life to the study of various martial arts and acupuncture to birth his own Needle Protocol and continues to make all his teaching accessible and easy to learn for all. (Search ITARA on Facebook)

- I leveraged all the teachers in my life and am continuously birthing, creating, reinventing, transforming, downloading, researching, learning, engineering, and hacking new ways to heal myself and share that with the world. I am never going to understand the Jungarian and abstract symbols like Raven will. I am never going to teach opening spiritual channels like Master Sha. I am never going to learn martial arts and TCM like Dr. Chu. But rather than feeling less than my teachers, I also know that none of them will integrate Shadow Work + Medical Intuition + Channeling to offer the kind of spiritual and science based, fun, creative, vulnerable shamanistic healing that I do.

My goal is to inspire you to become your own expression of the Tao. Remember, any time you are aware of feeling less than or more than someone, LAUGH and find compassion for your humanness, chant the mantra 我在道光中，道光在我中 (Wo Zai Dao Guang Zhong, Dao Guang Zai Wo Zhong = I am in the presence of Source Light, Source Light is radiating in me), then get yourself back into the arena and ask "Who do I get to be? What do I get to create now?"

I would be most honored to personally mentor and learn from anyone who wants to become their own unique kind of healer. #HackerHealer is so fun! I say YES to anyone who is willing to receive my love and offer me lessons!

FINAL WORD

Mother Teresa says, "if you want to change the world, go home and love your family." I say, "if you want to have harmony in the world, then please look inside your heart: start loving yourself, accepting yourself, and forgiving yourself."

Whatever labels we have assigned ourselves or others is rather empty. Let's say growing up, your dad said that you are irresponsible, disorganized, and messy. These three attributes are just conversations you continue to believe as true about yourself. When we do shadow work, we realize what he said about you is really a reflection of him. The truth is everybody has the same potential. I am just as "responsible, organized, or neat," or "irresponsible, disorganized and messy," as anybody else. These labels don't define us. We have moments when our behavior can be described as such, but all labels are empty. We are never stuck.

We are one. We all come from the same source, have the same roots, have the same potential for greatness and destruction.

The choice is ours. Live a disconnected life (me vs. others), or live a connected life (me and others). There is so much more joy, abundance, and gratitude when we choose love, belonging, and connection. Vulnerability is the birthplace of connection. Having the courage to do the shadow work requires us to take off our armor and look at the parts of us that we have been hiding from the world or ourselves.

We can't be authentic, powerful, and fully show up and own our gifts until we have owned our shadow.

Every shadow has a gift. There is truth in every shadow. By looking at our shadow, we can reduce our blind spots and see life as it is. One of the most important gifts in shadow work is cultivating our compassion muscle. When we can find compassion and rise above the mud for ourselves, we can find compassion for the suffering for all.

We can't be impeccable with our vibration unless we have met and embraced all our shadows. Instead of running away or cowering from our shadows, can we greet them? Accept them with a warm embrace? Loving them as much as we love our light?

To have no shadows means to have no light—the brighter your light, the darker your shadow. If shadow work is yin and chanting mantras is yang, then each time after we do shadow work, we balance with mantras. The best complement to the Ten Shadow is to trace the Tao Calligraphy of the Ten Da (www.DrSha.com).

When I started putting myself out there, leading meditation, or presenting at a conference, I would get crazy bouts of diarrhea. I am thankful for my diarrhea because the nervousness means that I am expanding outside of my comfort zone and taking risks! Diarrhea means I'm growing!

Can we reframe our pain as something to be composted rather than thrown away? By *composting* our pain, we are taking what was not serving us anymore and recycling it to feed us. Our pain is rich and nourishing with messages that feed our souls and aid our growth. *Pain is life's greatest teacher.*

The cancer patients I have all have one thing in common: they all have avoided, wallowed, and procrastinated facing their pain. Humans are "meaning-making machines." When we share our stories, we gain perspectives that help us see the emptiness of our pain. A lot of the time, we took on the pain from our ancestors or the collective!

Diana Miranda of Lifeworks Transformational Trainings says, "Events are neutral." It is our brains that make meaning and stay stuck in the details. Caroline Myss[2], expert in the fields of human consciousness, spirituality and mysticism, health, energy medicine, and the science of medical intuition, would tell us "get a bigger perspective by going on a higher floor."

Pain creates opportunities. That's basically what I do in my private practice. I enter your vibrational field and give attention to your pain. When we offer compassion to our pain, we can accept and release it with love, acknowledgment, and gratitude. Pain is our sacred clairsentient channel. It is a way our physical and emotional bodies give us a report card. Diana Miranda encouraged me to ask the question, "What do the results say?" What do the pains in our bodies say? Our body is a vehicle for enlightenment!

"Results come from showing up and putting in the repetitions OVER TIME (even when it's hard, and you don't feel like it.)" @lifeLikeLunden. Liberate your power today. Follow us on social media. Join our support groups. Sign up to take our classes. Watch the videos on YouTube.

---

1. Xiu, Master Rulin. *Divine Love: Divine Reveals How to Receive Divine Love, Abundance, Wisdom, Bliss and Beauty.* Rulin Xiu, 2014.
2. "About Caroline Myss." Caroline Myss, 26 July 2021, www.myss.com/about-caroline-myss.

4.2

JI'S GIFTS FROM SHADOW WORK

We all have our own unique expression of the Tao. It's like when my dad teaches me how to make kimchi. He can tell me and show me exactly what he does, but when I make it, my kimchi will be different from his. It would be my own. We each have unique fingerprints and have gifts to share with the world. The *way* we share our gifts will also be unique in their own expression.

Shadow work helps us find what our unique gifts are. Shadow work also aligns us closer to our soul's purpose.

SHAME HELPS BUILD MY COMPASSION MUSCLES

I am really good at wallowing in shame. I can live in a bath of shame and stay stuck in it for a long time. Shame is comforting in that in all the ways I have been able to tear others down, I have learned how to do it even more efficiently and meaner to myself. Shame has the very believable illusion of making you think you are worthless and so alone.

It is ironic that shame makes us feel incredibly lonely when all human beings have experienced shame.

While writing my dissertation on abortion stigma, I learned this: Shame is a universal feeling that is part of the human experience, yet the paradox of shame is that it can be isolating and lonely. Brené Brown, while researching *Shame Resilience Theory*[1], says that "We share in common what makes us feel the most apart."

The antidote to shame is compassion for yourself and for others. It is empathizing with others and yourself saying, "Hey. You are doing your best." But what happens when we tell ourselves that and we don't believe it? When there is still a voice in the back of our head that says, "But did you *really* try your best?" This is where shame spiraling starts.

It starts with all the ways I could have done my best. It continues with beating myself up over all the ways I could have done better and repeating the long list so that I hopefully don't forget, and next time I *will* be better. This was my tactic in trying to avoid another mistake in the future. I truly believed that if I drill it into myself long enough, I will learn and *never ever* do it again.

That is not true compassion. That is still punishing yourself and others, using shame as a teaching tactic. We do not learn well by punishment because that leads to living in fear. We get to fully integrate our lessons when we accept them lovingly into our hearts, not just our minds. This is why compassion takes practice. We get better at it as we do it more.

This is an adaptation to a Radiant Heart Meditation practice that I learned from Winnie, where she learned from her teacher Raven. Walk whatever needs you have to punish, and walk it into your heart. Walk your resentment, your anger, your shame, and your hatred into your heart. Your heart has an infinite amount of love, and nothing that you welcome into your heart can stay resistant to love. Eventually, your vengeance and your shame will turn into compassionate love. Whenever I have a hard time truly letting my self-compassion practice into my heart and continue doubting myself, I take that doubt and shame and accept it fully into my heart. All of it composts into love. I have to practice this daily, sometimes even on an hourly basis. As I consistently practice self-compassion and self-love, I have been better about getting off the rollercoaster of my shame cycles more quickly.

LEARNING THE IMPORTANCE OF COMPASSION *WITH* WISDOM

Compassion without wisdom is recklessness. For example, if I over identify with my mom's wounds, I become enmeshed and take on her wounds as if they are my own. Then I unnecessarily cause myself suffering. Compassion *with* wisdom is being able to get extremely close to the pain, fully love, and empathize, all while knowing that *every single person is capable of their own healing.*

When you take on and carry another's emotional baggage, you are not helping. First, you are sending out the message that you are much stronger than others, so you must carry their woes, eventually growing resentful and ungrateful. Second, you are *stealing* the other person's lesson and preventing them from awakening. You are not helping by trying to fix others. What you can do is love them fiercely, cheer them on while they excavate each painful wound, listen compassionately without judgment, and believe in their own healing journey.

Even if my mom may have caused me pain, she cannot take it away. Only I can heal me. Only she can heal herself. Compassion with wisdom is being able to truly listen with love and understanding, knowing that one's own journey is their own. Self-compassion is being able to honor and listen to oneself with no judgment, only with full love and acceptance.

APPRECIATING STRONG 정 (JEONG)

There are many Korean words that cannot be translated into English. Words like 눈치 (noonchi or nunchi) and 띠동갑 (ttee-dong-kab). The Korean word 정 (Jeong) is one that has multiple layers of meaning that even I am still deciphering to this day. Jeong is a concept where there is a warm energy of connection being exchanged between two people. It's like when there is an energetic bond of two hearts that develops over time.

To confuse you even further, Jeong could be used to describe individuals and their own energetic fields. If someone has a lot of Jeong, their warm energy emanates from them in a noticeable way. Some individuals have deep Jeong, which means their Jeong is saved for their loved ones running a strong current deep in their heart. Then there's a specific Jeong created between two individuals, where maybe they were not fond of each other at first, but through bickering and playful fighting, connection and Jeong occurred. Jeong is hard to explain because it is cultural and because it is something that is *felt* and not said.

As a Korean American, I learned about Jeong later in life from my aunts and family in Korea. The biggest compliment I got was from one of my aunts. She said that I am someone who has a lot of Jeong, emanating a warm energy from my being. I take that compliment deeply into my heart because that was not always the case. From my childhood traumas, I learned to survive by giving out a "don't you dare mess with me" energy. Throughout my emotional and spiritual growth, that protective survival shell has been peeled off layer by layer. With every year I age wiser, I grow more into my real self. It's ironic that part of growing up is first getting pretty far from yourself to survive and fit in, then coming back to yourself by unlearning patterns that were once crucial.

The beautiful thing about Jeong is the importance of a collectivistic connection. Jeong cannot happen unless both people participate in the connection and energy. Collectivistically, all the Jeong shared between people in our homes, communities, sisterhoods, families, and society raises *all* of our consciousness.

There is a strong Jeong between Winnie and me. It is our powerful and tender Jeong that started a sisterhood that also birthed this book. I hope that as you have been reading along and learning about our stories, you have been opening your heart to us and creating Jeong with the people in your life. I hope Jeong is radiating strongly in your relationships with others, and especially the relationship you have with yourself. My intention for this book is to show you how I've gotten closer to myself in the process of doing shadow work, with the hopes that it inspires you in your own journey.

HEALING WOUNDS AND DISCOVERING MORE

Shadow work is really hard. But there is beauty in shadow work because it helps us heal our deepest wounds. There is a difference between wounds and triggers. If our life is seen as a journey through a vast landscape, there has been an obsession in our current culture to walk through life without stepping on any landmines. People will say "don't trigger me" or "that is too triggering." There is this craving to avoid triggers, or landmines, at all costs. But triggers are opportunities to heal the wound. Triggers are when salt is being poured into our wounds. We are going around demanding that others don't throw salt on our wounds, when in reality, life is salt. Salt is everywhere. If you heal the wound, however much salt is thrown at you, it won't burn.

It is through the shadow work that we look deeply at our infected, pus-filled wound, and perform surgery. We stitch the wound back up, braiding each thread with love and self-compassion, and letting the wound fully heal. Shadow work is not a one and done process. As you heal one wound, you will discover more. It is a lifelong process and it is rewarding just as much as it is painful. As someone who is on the path, I can guarantee that it is a thousand percent worth it. By doing shadow work, I get to welcome triggers into my life with openness and understanding.

Don't resist every trigger and surrender to the process. Surrendering will get you closer to freedom and liberation.

"The moment of surrender is not when life is over, it's when it begins."

— Marianne Williamson

ALIGNING TO MY SOUL'S PURPOSE

As I unfold and discover another layer of myself, I have become more conscious and aligned to what my purpose is. I know that one of my missions in this life is to spread the wealth of the wisdom and lessons I have gained so far. I strongly believe in sharing to raise *all* of our consciousness. I don't believe in hoarding any new wisdom or aha moments of discovery.

Another purpose I have is to be the microphone to talk about all the taboo topics that many individuals spend lifetimes avoiding. I know that I am here to *go there* with people to places people don't normally go, or want to go. Topics of abortion, murder, shame, disgust, envy, anger, fear, and unworthiness are not favorite party conversation starters. However, I know that I get to use my courage to be able to shed a spotlight on what is taboo. I get to use my gifts to serve in my purpose.

I still don't know exactly *how* my purpose will unfold, but I trust that it will blossom in Divine timing.

LEARNING NATURE'S PRESENCE

Nature is the Tao. Nature just is. Nature doesn't judge and say the rose is beautiful while labeling the tiger eating the rabbit as cruel. We humans are the ones that create meaning over the yin and yang, and the essence of nature. We are part of nature and we must learn that we also have seasons and cycles. We are all constantly living in the presence of impermanence.

In Chapter 2 of Tao Te Ching:

"When people see some things as beautiful,

other things become ugly.

When people see some things as good,

other things become bad.

Being and non-being create each other.

Difficult and easy support each other.

Long and short define each other.

High and low depend on each other.

Before and after follow each other.

Therefore the Master

acts without doing anything

and teaches without saying anything.

Things arise and she lets them come;

things disappear and she lets them go.

She has but doesn't possess,

acts but doesn't expect.

When her work is done, she forgets it.

That is why it lasts forever."

---

1. Brown, B. (2006). Shame resilience theory: A grounded theory study on women and shame. Families in Society, 87(1), 43–52. https://doi.org/10.1606/1044-3894.3483

4.3

THE GIFT OF AWAKENING TO THE GREATEST LOVE FROM BIRTHING THIS BOOK: 1+1=3

When we put Ji's and Winnie's stories together, 1+1=3. The remainder of this book is about the magic that is created from the magic between Winnie and Ji, from Winnie's perspective:

THE MAGIC BETWEEN WINNIE AND JI

I am so grateful to Ji for being the co-author of this book. 1+1=3 because there is Winnie's magic, Ji's magic, and the magic between us.

Being a mother on the receiving end of the alienation, when Ji would tell me the things she had said to her mom, my heart would break, but also a part of me found such deep compassion for her mom's suffering. I was the recipient of "You are not my mom, I don't want a relationship with you, you have no right to ask me any questions." The helplessness I felt for what seemed like eternal darkness, where no matter how hard I tried, my daughter would not talk to me. I thought she hated me. I hated myself. So, I asked Ji to tell me about her story. "Tell me more about how you repaired with your mom. Tell me how you went back to loving your mom. Tell me about your dad." I knew that I would find comfort in her story.

The part of her story when she questioned how could she have negative feelings for someone who is so loving, the part of the story when she said she could see the grief pouring out of her mother's eyes, I know that isn't just her voice. That is also the voice of my children. How much must it have pained my daughter to say those hurtful words to reject the very person who loved her the most? How much poison is in my beloved children's bodies? How much internal conflict is happening inside them? Oh how I long to go hug my daughter and comfort her and tell her that everything is going to be okay. How I long to drink the poison out of her body. How I long for her to let me help her process her poison? How much I wanted to help her in her pain. But she just won't let me in—It killed me inside. I speak about this, regardless of whether you have ever had a divorce or if you have ever been rejected by your own children when they needed help the most. How completely utterly helpless and powerless and dark to be isolated from your child? How much shame I felt knowing that I was responsible for part of the poison that went into my child?

JI'S PERSPECTIVE HELPED ME APPRECIATE MY CHILDREN

For months I tortured myself as a victim, repeating the same conversation, "How can they alienate me, push me away, when all I ever did was love them?" It was not until Ji's story that I understood how hard it is to be the children of divorce. How it is child abuse to force your children to pick a side. How saying anything negative to your child about the other parent kills your child inside.

Ji's story about being parentified also helped me realize what a tremendous gift my other daughter, who was parentified, gave me. While one daughter went into alienating me, my other daughter became the glue, the therapist, trying to help her dad, her sister, and her mom process the divorce. There were days when she was the only person who watched TV with me in silence on the couch. There were days I cried under the disguise of the TV drama, when I was actually drowning in my own grief. There were days when asking me to drive her to Starbucks for a coffee or going to Target for a binder was all the human interaction I got. Ji's story about sitting in silence with her mom at the restaurant for an hour reminded me of the countless meals and car rides my daughters and I had in silence. The awkwardness of them not speaking, nor I. I couldn't open my mouth either, fearing that I would just crumble into a pond of tears. I didn't want to burden my children, I didn't want to frighten my children, and I didn't want to let my grief out. So I kept everything inside and just didn't talk to them. Going through the divorce was hard enough, and shutting my mouth was a way of holding back my tears.

I am so grateful for having an empathic daughter who was the rock for the family and me. Thank goodness she kept me alive. This is the gift of stepping up during challenging times. To all the children who had to parent their parents, thank you for being there for your parents. To all the parents who have gone through a divorce, please know that the love a child has for their parents is unconditional, and nothing in the world can break the parent-child bond.

Parental alienation and parental competition, "trying to be the preferred parent," forces our children to take sides and judge the parents with their brains instead of connecting with their hearts.

While you may not be engaging in parental alienation such as changing the telephone number, you may be engaging in parental competition—trying to "outdo" the other parent so that your children love you more, or think that you are the better parent, or that you are the more fun parent. STOP. There is no need to compete as to who makes the better breakfast, who buys the better Christmas presents, or who takes them on the more fun vacations. I get it. After you lose your significant other, the natural inclination is that you hold on to your children even tighter. You need your children's love and their approval even more than ever because it feels like that is all you have. Please know any kind of hate, resentment, anger, competition, comparison, and judgment between parents TEARS your children apart.

The only thing children ever truly want is to see their dad happy and their mom happy and balanced. By the way, any effort to sabotage the other's relationship simply doesn't work. When divorced parents don't have a loving, supportive, friendly relationship, they force their children to lie and hide. Children can't really share how they feel because it is not safe for them to share. If my child had shared about how happy she was while she was on vacation with dad, she would be afraid that the truth would make me sad. If my child had shared about how depressing it is at the other house, she would also be afraid that the truth would make me sad. There was nothing my child could have said to me, good or bad, that didn't make me sad. That story of Ji sitting in silence with her mom, not knowing what to say, was exactly how I felt with my daughters so many times.

PARENT-CHILD BOND CANNOT BE BROKEN

One time John almost sabotaged my MLK day breakfast with my kids by cooking a big breakfast and telling the kids ahead of time, even though the agreement that was clearly stated in the text message chat room was that I would take the kids out to breakfast before dropping them off. When my child told me she didn't want to eat breakfast with me, she saw the look of grief that came out of my eyes and decided to eat two breakfasts. First with me, then with dad. But she tried to hide the guest and gathering that was happening at John's house. She didn't want me to be sad. When I had to grab some old belongings from the house, I walked in on John making the big breakfast. Janeen said, "Oops. You're not supposed to be here." I saw another adult woman's shoes, and I saw another car.

My children kept things from me to protect me. I wish they knew that the truth might hurt, but it also heals and liberates. It is in sharing, not hiding that the healing takes place. One time I had a client cry on my treatment table as she confessed her deepest shame, that she had learned how to hurt her mom from her dad. Her shame confession was the greatest medicine because I was that mom.

We don't heal by keeping things to ourselves. Just like within every teacher is a student, within every student is a teacher. Within every parent is a child, within every child is a parent. Every child loves their parents unconditionally and teaches, guides, and supports their parents' journey. This is the principle that yin is constantly transforming to yang, and yang is constantly transforming to yin. Our children love us, guide us and protect us, as much as we love them, guide them and protect them.

P.S. As I read Ji's chapter on Inner Child, I wondered where mine was. Maybe recovering my inner child would be a future book.

CHILDREN LOVE, SUPPORT, AND PROTECT THEIR PARENTS

I didn't want to lean on my kids as my therapists, but the truth is, I have leaned on both of them for comfort. In the darkest days of my life, when John used to yell at me constantly, I would put my younger daughter on my chest to "comfort her and put her to bed," but the reality was that she was the one that was comforting me. Silent tears rolled down my face and wet her pillow for countless nights.

Going between two houses is not easy, but from the deepest part of my heart, I thank my kids every day for the sacrifices they make to see both parents. As I cry writing this, I know I am one of the luckiest ones who gets to see my kids six days a week. (I worked out a 50/50 deal where I get my kids Sunday, Tuesday, and Thursday nights, and Monday, Wednesday, and Friday mornings).

No parent ever wants to hurt their children. No parent ever wants to disconnect their children from their hearts and scar them from having trusting, nourishing relationships. Thank goodness for the unconditional love that both my daughters gave me. Whether they gave me hostility that led to my awakening, or they gave me their requests for cooking, I am so appreciative of them.

I used to judge myself as a bad parent if my kids were on the screens too much, watching too much TV, or playing too much video games. Having been through the hardest year of minimal communication with my kids, I can honestly say thank GOD for TV, thank GOD for video games, thank GOD for screens and Wifi, because having the three of us sitting in silence, watching TV together or playing on our own respective device, is a freaking treasure. Every breath that we share under the same roof is simply precious. Even having them playing video games in a locked bedroom is precious! Anything is better than me alone in a house with no other human's qi or heartbeat.

EVERY TALK THERAPIST AND EVERY FAMILY OF DIVORCE SHOULD READ THIS BOOK

Truly, every talk therapist or healer should read this book and prescribe this book to any parent or child who has gone through a divorce (who is old enough for the content of this book). The perspectives of the divorced parent and the divorced child help us find compassion, forgiveness, and closure. We forgive, not because the other person deserves pardon, but because we deserve true peace.

I am almost certain there will be a future book dedicated to repairing friendships and parent-child bonds.

THE GIFT OF AWAKENING TO GOD AND LOVE FROM JOHN, MY PARENTS, THE KIDS, AND ME

Expressing all that helplessness as a mother, desperately wanting to connect with her children, helped me understand the depth of John's love for me. For six years, I cried in my own room, shutting him out from my pain. I kept myself isolated and didn't let him love me. The same way my daughters wanted to protect me from the truth, keep me in the dark and not tell me anything, was the same way I wanted to protect John from the truth, keep him in the dark and not tell him anything.

There is one last part to the story of the divorce. Two weeks before we decided to separate, Jay and I had completely terminated our romantic relationship with each other. Jay's ancestors had told him that our relationship could not continue because it was splitting Winnie in two directions, it wasn't good for Jay to be an extra in the John and Winnie relationship, and it wasn't fair to John. It was painful for everyone involved, but it was important for us to return to our integrity.

During this same time, I had just connected to my ancestral karma, and the three weeks leading up to the decision to divorce, I was crying alone in my bedroom, all day and every day, undergoing what we call spiritual purification. John felt that no matter how hard he tried, he was disconnected from me. And he was right.

It was ME that was emotionally unavailable. It was ME that shut him out. It was ME that didn't let him love me. It was ME that didn't trust the God in him to be able to be a safe place for me to turn to.

When John said, "I wish you had turned to me instead of suffering alone," that was God speaking to me through John. All these years, God witnessed all my tears, grief, agony, suppression, fear, unworthiness, and conflicts. All these years, God has been loving me, supporting me, and protecting me through John, my teachers, my parents, and my kids. It was ME who shut everybody out. It was ME who didn't receive God and love from everyone. Because I didn't know God in me, I couldn't see, receive and appreciate the God in all.

Everyone loves me when I let them in. I now let everyone have all of me, the light and the shadows.

P.S. The reason I was able to have an awakening through my crisis was that I had the honor of being a reader, a client, and a student of Dr. Raven Lee's work on "Unbinding the Soul: Awakening through crisis." The reason I met Raven was a referral from Evelyn. I met Evelyn as a referral from John's therapist Amy. So at the end of the day, John was the giver of my awakening! (No John, no Raven, no initiation and guidance on the spiritual path). This also illustrates the butterfly effect, that we never know the impact of a referral or an encounter.

Connection, connection, connection. Life is a connection and relationship game.

P.P.S Terry McGill once gave me a reading that my lesson was to learn the Greatest Gratitude from John, and John's lesson was to learn the Greatest Love from me. As it turns out, all the support I wanted from God has been available to me all along (and will be available to me the rest of my life), and all the love John wanted has been available to him all along (and will be available to him the rest of his life). I am so blessed for all the guidance Terry has offered over the years. Here's how you contact him: Terry@heartandsoulservices.org

P.P.P.S Actually, everyone who wants to awaken should read this book, not just those whose lives have been impacted by a divorce!!!!

4.4

TURNING MY DARKNESS INTO SAFETY AND KINDNESS

LEARNING TO LOVE MYSELF

I feel like there are gold and hard-earned lessons in every paragraph and every chapter of this book. I know I will be reading this book and coming back to it as a resource even 30 years later. As I prepare myself for podcasts and interviews, I ask myself, if there can only be one takeaway for you and for me—what is it?

⇒ Learning how to take off the armor, open my heart, and let everyone in, including me, to love myself.

In this book, I told you about all the mistakes I have made—shadow work is really about finding love, mercy, and kindness when we least deserve it. What is the truth?

• The truth was that on March 8, 2019, I made a promise to myself that I would never hurt myself or my family again by cheating.

- The truth was that I wore baggy clothes, avoided eye contact, and was not looking for any relationships outside the marriage.

- The truth was that I ignored the red flags of how uncomfortable I felt by Jay's gaze. If I were in touch with my anger, I would have gotten angry and set boundaries. Because I was disconnected from my anger, I doubted myself and talked myself out of feeling angry. "Nothing is wrong with him, it's me, I'm too sensitive, what's wrong with me for feeling uncomfortable?"

- The truth was that Jay, John, and I all played a role in breaking up my family and causing grief to John, me, and my kids.

- The truth was that John, me, and my kids have every right to be angry at the ego in John, me, and Jay for being the perpetrators that caused trauma to our family.

Kari Kampakis @karikampakis shared in her Instagram post, "Religion is 'I messed up, my dad is gonna kill me.' Gospel is 'I messed up, I need to call my Dad.'" It's our rock bottom moments that open the door to God's mercy. As Father Joseph Corpora says, "God saves us through our sins, through our imperfections, through our faults, through our failings, through our weaknesses. God saves us as sinners, not as saints."

Bingo. I'm here to admit my mistakes and let God carry me. I love myself, not because I deserve it, but because God loves me unconditionally. No matter how much I have sinned, God never stops loving me. The more I open my heart, the more I ask God to come into my heart, the more I can be healed and share myself with the world.

For years, I walked around with "Men are assholes" and "Women are bitches". What I now realize is that all the armor I wore never protected me from suffering. The people who took advantage of me did, the people who abandoned me did. The armor did not protect me from heartbreaks. What the armor did do was prevent me from having intimacy with myself and kept me from going to them for love or for help. The armor was actually counterproductive and caused more traumas and disconnection. I still have a lot more work to do in dropping my defenses, opening my heart, and surrendering to God's plan for me. Will you join me in learning how to have intimacy with God, with ourselves, and then with the rest of the world?

THE CLEAN BREAKUP

The more I let go of my People Pleaser, the more I am in touch with my sacred anger, the more clarity I get. It was not until writing this book that I saw the way Jay entered into my life by getting through my defenses. Of course, my lack of boundaries, the loneliness of social isolation during Covid, my disconnection with John and the kids were also at play, but Jay definitely played a role in breaking my family. The more I allowed myself to see how I have been a victim, the more I also saw how I was also a perpetrator in taking advantage of Jay's kindness, nourishment, and caretaking. He did the job of loving myself for me, and I took advantage of the energy that he eagerly poured into me.

I thank Jay and myself wholeheartedly for all the love and support we poured into each other. I also thank both of us for all the ways we helped each other grow. Before our first energy exchange, he was uncertain of his healing gifts, and I was uncertain of my spiritual channels. He had put me on a pedestal, I had also put him on a pedestal, and both of our unworthiness created unhealthiness in our lives. He tried to prove himself useful to me while I tried to earn the affection of my kids. We were both people-pleasers, and we were both perpetrators.

Closure happens when we know, "What is it that I learned from this relationship?" As Stefanos @stefanossifandos, the relationship coach, says, "Forgiveness is freeing and feeling. In order to forgive freely, we must feel. In the feeling is where the *release takes place*. That's where we disempower them and empower ourselves. And in the sense of empowerment is where we grow. That's where we learn more about our boundaries in the world. That is how we learn to say No and say Yes."

In the beginning months of COVID, John imposed a strict lockdown, and neither he nor the kids wanted to spend time with me. Like so many others that went on antidepressants or consumed alcohol, without the support of my family and friends, I went back to my old addictions of enjoying attention from someone I'm not "supposed to". Looking back, Jay was the greatest gift that God sent me. Jay filled an attachment need that nobody else in my life was showing up for. About two months after the divorce, I opened my heart to Jay. With my whole heart, I thank Jay for being the rescuer and the many happy memories we have together.

This is the magic of 1+1=3. Reading Ji's story, I realized how Ji wanted her mom to choose her daughter over Mom's Dude, which is how my kids want me to choose them. While I forgave Jay, I don't know that John or my kids can forgive him as easily. If being "one family under two roofs" is what I want to manifest for my family, letting go of Jay, no matter how much I love him, is what is in the highest and best interest of my family and ultimately me. I need to take some space being single —do the job of loving myself without outsourcing to anyone—before I can show up in any conscious relationship. I love how every heartbreak has become an opportunity to further open my heart and show up more fully.

My TCM teacher says the best way to break up is to gently untie the knot like you would untie your shoelaces. That way, both people leave feeling whole. Never cut with a knife or scissors. The silent treatment leaves an open wound and permanent damage. The clean breakup that I had with Jay is a testament to the shadow work that we both do. We can have difficult conversations and leave each other with our hearts fully open to each other, remain close friends, and continue to collaborate as partners in our healing work.

BREAKING THE CYCLE

Seeing my daughter not love herself breaks my heart.

A divorce is like death to the kids. "I am not worthy of my parents' love. If my parents loved me enough, they would choose me. They would choose to be with me, not 50/50, but 100% of the time. How can my mother choose another dude over me? How can my dad give up on doing the work to keep the family together? Why can't my mother love herself enough? Why can't my dad go to therapy with mom and give up on the family?"

When they grow older, they may have compassion and understand the incompatibility, mom's addiction, or dad's fear that led to the divorce.

The child that gets angry and lashes out at everything—is doing well. She is in touch with her voice and ability to express her feelings. The child that goes numb or denies her feelings is disconnecting and experiencing soul loss. I saw the light go out in my people-pleasing daughter. It kills me inside, and I can only imagine what Ji's mom felt like seeing her skinny daughter lose so much weight. I can only imagine Ji's pain in wishing her mom would come back to her.

When we say, "Don't stay together for the kids, the kids will be okay,"—yes, there is some truth to that. Of course, everyone will be okay. But let's not pretend that the children of divorce did not undergo tremendous trauma. The children adopt a coping mechanism in order to survive. They build heart walls and disconnect with themselves.

I finally understand why my angry daughter said she felt like she didn't matter. Because I didn't choose her. But I couldn't have chosen her, because I never chose me. I didn't love myself. It was not until writing this book did I realize—I never chose myself. Since the first time I was suicidal at eight, I never chose myself.

I am committing to loving and honoring myself because how I love and honor myself is how my daughters will love and honor themselves and me. I am determined to set a good example for them.

LETTING MYSELF GET ANGRY IS AN ACT OF SELF-LOVE

Writing this book, I finally discovered something. Sure, others may have taken advantage of my kindness as a perpetrator, but I have been a perpetrator to myself, more than anyone has. I am the one who has shut myself down and denied myself more than anyone. It was ME that constantly talked myself out of being angry. Have you ever said *"Don't get mad"* to yourself? How often do I invalidate my feelings?

The most important relationship is the one with ourselves. Say YES to ourselves. Learn to receive the totality of our experience. Instead of "Don't get mad," how about "I see that I am mad. Can I embrace conflicts as opportunities to deepen connection and intimacy? Let's open my heart and have a conversation. Give my anger a voice and listen with the intent to understand. I am so grateful for the sacred voice of my anger for sharing because all perspectives matter, and I want to honor my anger."

I am so grateful to Jay for facilitating the soul retrieval that helped me reconnect with my anger. I have struggled with boundaries my whole life because my anger has been suppressed. Anger is protection. Anger helps us have clarity. Anger roots from love because we care. As a lifetime people-pleasing mom, I cannot tell you the number of times I have denied and suppressed my anger when my kids are being disrespectful, and I just kept stuffing my anger into my body. I cannot tell you the number of parenting books, parenting coaches, and parenting support groups I have done over the years. While it has been tremendously valuable to learn from all the experts, get 1:1 coaching and be part of a support group—nobody can tell me the "best" way to parent because if it doesn't come from me, it is not authentic. My kids don't need a good mom, they need an authentic mom. Good moms raise people pleasers (monkey see, monkey do). Authentic moms raise authentic kids.

When Ji told me she had to let go of the goal of ever getting off her medication, I was so grateful for her teaching. As Ji's mentor, I was tempted to tell Ji that for as long as she is taking meds, she is tempering with the clarity of her brain and not honoring the original perfection that God gave her. I never said anything to her because deep in my heart, I knew that I didn't know better than Ji. I want Ji to always trust herself and not let anyone tell her she is wrong. So, I opened my heart to being Ji's student, that while some people are able to graduate from meds, some people stay on meds forever, and that is okay! As Ji's student, Ji told me that as long as she had "getting off meds" as a goal, she was setting herself up for an impossible standard, like women trying to look like a swimsuit model 36-24-36. How many years did it take me to love my body, just the way it is? I want to take a moment to pat myself on the back for being the humble mentor-student that I am because instead of lecturing to Ji about what I know, I allowed her to teach me something I didn't know: By having a goal of an "ideal parent", it is going to be impossible for me to love myself as I am. I am me. I am the way that I am. I can't be someone I am not. I don't want to live my life focusing on "What's wrong with me." I want to spend more time focusing on "What's perfect with this moment?"

As much as I want to become "unconditional love" to my kids, I realized I must let go of my attachment to ever getting there. I have decided to let go of denying my anger when my kids are being rude. I choose to be unapologetically myself and accept the perfection that is in the present moment. I give up struggling and trust my kids will open their hearts to me in divine timing.

UNBINDING THE NEGATIVE KARMA

> "The silent treatment is so painful to experience because we learn that when we upset someone, we no longer exist to them." Dr. Nicole LePera @the.holistic.psychologist.

When we receive emotional abuse or when we are in a toxic relationship, is there a kinder way to take space without making the other person feel shame and abandoned for doing something wrong? Is there a way to make the other person feel deeply loved instead of punished? Is there a way to stay connected but disarm the other person from the toxic behavior?

The way I ghosted Mr. Intoxicating, I know I might have given him scars and left him feeling wounded. The way John cut me off and blocked communication with me made me feel utterly worthless and devastated. Well, you can say, "he deserved it because he raped," or "I deserved it because I cheated." You can say, "that's your negative karma! You get what you sow."

Remember, we are more connected beyond our wildest imagination. We all drink from the same river. One person cleans the river, and it benefits everyone. One person pollutes the river, and it poisons everyone. The way I ghosted or the way I received silent treatment were both perpetuating the negative karma, passing from one relationship to another. Break up traumas spread from one relationship to the next, like ancestral karma is passed from one generation to the next. Sure, we can find compassion for perpetuating the pain because "we have done our best," but perhaps there is a way to tap into mercy, unbinding the knot, releasing the negative karma, and spreading positive karma.

During the writing process, Ji shared how she was abusive towards her mom, "I am going to hurt you by disappearing and not telling you where I went, just the way you hurt dad by disappearing and not telling him where you went." The act of Ji taking ownership of her manipulation is the best healing balm that soothes my pain as a mom. The way she hurt her mom is being **composted into medicine** for healing my trauma. When *vulnerability in sharing is present*, we can *heal darkness with darkness*.

Because Ji and I own and know our darkness of manipulation, we can spot and know another's darkness of manipulation. In yoga, we say, "the light in me, sees the light in you." Well, **the darkness in us, sees the darkness in all.**

By doing all the shadow work, we learned how to make peace with reality, accept what is already here, and let go of seeking for what may never be there.

WHEN WE HIT ROCK BOTTOM IN OUR SHADOW WORK, IT'S TIME TO BRING IN THE LIGHT

Shadow is a very dark place. A lot of people are scared of shadow work because they are afraid they will get stuck and can't get out. This is the time to practice mantras and call in the love and light. Remember, dark is followed by light, and light is followed by dark. This is nature's way.

Don't do shadow work alone! Shadow work can be a place for building trust and intimacy. Either do it with a professional who specializes in shadow work in the human physical realm or do it with spiritual guides. I never do any shadow work without calling a guide because I want someone to hold my hand the entire time and carry me out of the tunnel.

SEEING THE PERFECTION IN ALL

After we decided to divorce, I asked John, "If I had cancer and I was dying in less than 12 months, would you still want a divorce?" The answer was no. His answer reveals that the root cause of the divorce isn't that we don't love each other enough. It's a tragic clash of egos. There is something worth celebrating: the fact that he chose to leave me meant that I was strong enough to take care of myself. He would never leave me if I had cancer, if I was crippled, or if I was blind. John is a channel of God, delivering lessons for me when I am ready to handle them.

Remember, there are infinite ways to interpret events. Events are neutral. If I label them as emotional abuse, if I want to be right about being a victim, well, then I am right. At the textbook level, I am a victim of complex PTSD, and I ping pong between triggers. I can choose to stay here, in the suffering, or I can give up the attachment of being right about the labels.

Do I want to be right about having complex PTSD? Do I want to be right about being a victim of emotional abuse? Do I want to be loved and to love?

Sometimes in a relationship, we enter **_gridlock_**. It came down to my fear of abandonment vs. his fear of abandonment, my defensiveness vs. his defensiveness. I don't trust him not to hurt me again vs. he doesn't trust me not to hurt him again. I don't want to let him into my heart vs. he doesn't want to let me into his heart.

There is a part of me that wants to withdraw and not have intimacy again. (Diana Miranda calls this "taking the ball home and not play with others"). But an even bigger part of me craves to have a profoundly intimate connection with others.

That is why it's helpful to work with Jesus and St. Francis, "seek not to be loved, but to love. Seek not to be understood, but to understand." The ultimate goal of shadow work isn't to diagnose me with "what's wrong." It's to validate my victim with compassion and then find mercy. I find mercy because God gave me mercy first. Ask God for the courage to show up and love again. Ask God to fill me with patience until the conflicts resolve. Ask God for protection, strength, and guidance.

The only way to graduate from trauma is to delete all the labels. I laugh because that is a kind of manipulation, that is a kind of self invalidation. I am basically trying to talk myself out of being a victim. But then, would I rather be right and stay in victimhood, or would I rather go love and be loved? Would I rather have heart walls and trust nobody, or do I choose to go back to the arena and experience love with no armor? I choose to be kind because I want to be kind to myself, and I want the world to be a kinder place.

HEALING THE SOURCE WOUND "I DON'T MATTER"

In writing this book, there were times when I doubted myself as an author. "Am I too wordy? Is this too long? Am I wasting my reader's time? Do I sound like a broken record? Is there any way I can shorten the book?"

I reflected on why I was so hard on myself as an author, and I discovered some gems:

1) I am really grateful for the way I have parented my kids. While I expected excellence for myself, I never demanded performance from my kids. I wasn't going to be critical of my kids like my mom was to me, and I am so proud of myself for that. :)

2) There is insecurity about being a writer. I have made up conversations about English not being my native language, and also, none of my degrees required extensive writing.

3) I have a core fear of being big, being seen, being heard, taking up space, and taking up other people's time.

Ah ha! One of my source fractures is that "I don't matter, and I don't want to be a bother or an inconvenience to others."

Instead of reading this book with the filter of "what's wrong with me," I choose to read it with "what's perfect about me." This book is perfectly imperfect. This book is authentically our voice, and there is no price in this world that is worth compromising our authenticity.

NO ONE IS TOO MUCH, AND EVERYONE'S VOICE NEEDS TO BE HEARD

I am most grateful to Ji and Jay for always listening to me, always believing in me, and always saying "Yes" to me, especially when I was suppressing myself, not trusting myself, and not loving myself. This book could not have happened without your support.

I really thank Jay for reading every chapter as it came out and finding all parts of the book necessary. I also thank him for being my trash can for all the times when my poison needed to be emptied. Jay is a shamanic archeologist, and I really appreciate the compassionate inquiry he uses to help me dive deeper into my poison. He can do remote sessions too! He's a good digger. (www.shamanicalchemy.site)

WANT TO WRITE YOUR OWN BOOK?

I highly recommend my book coach, Sandra Rodriguez Bicknell of Soulfully Aligned Publishing. Thank you, Sandra, for being my book coach. Not only did she guide me through the sacred process of birthing this book, but she saw my divinity and made me feel like I am a gift and that I have something to give to the universe from Day 1. More important than the book coaching was healing the source fracture that I don't matter. Everyone should seriously work with Sandra to birth your story. (Sandra@SoulfullyAlignedPublishing.com)

The process of writing a book is so healing. From "Master Storytelling: How to Turn Your Experiences Into Stories that Teach, Lead, and Inspire" by Mark J. Carpenter and Darrell D. Harmon, stories are a great tool to teach, lead and inspire, because "stories activate the amygdala, a part of the brain near the brain's 'storage unit'." The vividness of the story, plus the emotional impact of it, create memorable experiences for listeners."

Thank you to Colleen for formatting and editing our book so beautifully. Ji and my stories came to life because of her loving efficiency and gifts. (PublishingStrategyInfo@gmail.com)

My dear shaman friend, Ada Trinh, came up to me the first time she attended my Integrated Healing Circle and told me that I am a sage and told me that I would be living the life of a sage. Can you imagine what it is like to have a stranger walk up to you and tell you that you are meant to be a sage? Get a clarity reading with her (www.shamanada.com).

Owning my Own Magic

Last but not least, I thank myself for being a gift to myself, my kids, my family, my clients, and the world. Trauma is the separation from love. Divorce and parental alienation are the most traumatic experiences. Nothing hurts the psyche more than to be rejected by our loved ones *by choice*. I thank myself for turning the greatest pain into my greatest power. I used my life's trauma to open my heart further, which increased my spiritual healing power exponentially. As Master Sha teaches, "The love from our hearts melt all blockages and transform all life."

When Ji shared her story of her jealousy of my powers, I asked myself, how did I overcome the jealousy of my teachers? How did I stop putting my teachers on pedestals? How did I stop comparing myself to my teachers? And that is when I gained clarity on the tremendous gift I got from Dr. Chu:

I am so blessed to have the three most important ShiFu in my life: Raven, Master Sha, and Dr. Chu. Raven initiated me on my spiritual path, and Master Sha helped me integrate spiritual healing into the evidence-based medicine I was already practicing. Still, it was Dr. Chu who gave me the most priceless gift: his humanity and authenticity gave me the *permission to be me*. He gave me *confidence* and *trust* in myself. He is the one who helped me overcome the fear of making mistakes. Nobody is born knowing how to diagnose, how to prescribe herbs, and perform acupuncture. No successful healer did not start from making mistakes and learning from them. Dr. Chu is a true warrior, and I am so grateful he helped me show up in the arena. Dr. Chu was the one who repeatedly told me that *I didn't need anyone's permission to be me.*

Diana Miranda's Lifeworks Transformation programs also helped me go "all-in". She also has programs for teenagers, which I pray my daughters will take.
(www.lifeworksworldwide.com)

I hope you also give yourself permission to own the "Fierce Light of the Universe" that you are meant to be. Shoutout to Journey 54 and everyone who loves me, supports me, and helps me spread love and healing to this world!

STAY TUNED

I hope that my next collaborative book, "The Tao of Integrative Healing", will go further into detail about how I integrate Soul + Heart + Mind + Energy + Body into helping my clients heal.

• Soul - Master Sha's Tao Calligraphy Healing (or chanting mantras)

• Heart - Raven's Radiant Heart Meditations (or breathing compassion in the heart)

• Mind - Diana's Lifeworks Transformation mindset shifts (or deleting limiting conversations)

• Energy - acupuncture + Dr. Chu's channel diagnosis (or energy moving practices)

• Body - Yoga, posture, body alignment (or body moving practices)

明 "ming" (to understand, to illuminate, to have clarity)

日 "ri" (the sun, the yang)

月 "yue" (the moon, the yin)

The word 明 to understand, to illuminate, to have clarity is made up of two words: the sun and the moon. It is only when we bring the yin and yang together that we get the complete picture.

If you enjoyed the yin yang of this book, we are going to bring the "everything is a gift" perspective to DSM in a future book. Do you want to know about the impermanence of anxiety and depression? The gifts of anxiety and depression? The yin and yang transformation between anxiety and depression? How to exit the suffering of anxiety and depression? Stay tuned!

As we are constantly evolving and reinventing, by the time you read this book, we will have healed a deeper layer. Please subscribe to our social media and YouTube channels for the most up to date downloads of mediations and transformational exercises.

Website: www.MindfulHealingHeart.com
Instagram: www.Instagram.com/HonoringDarkness
www.Instagram.com/MindfulHealingHeart
Facebook: www.Facebook.com/MindfulHealingHeart
Youtube: www.YouTube.com/c/MindfulHealingHeart

We will be hosting workshops, private support groups and offering both free and paid content to support your discovery of your Ten Greatest Shadows!

4.5

MESSAGE FROM SPIRIT

Dear one,

You are already there. Let go of everything in the past. Enjoy the present moment and everyone in your life right now. Your time together is very short. Treasure every moment.

Peace is here when you stop seeking. The more we share our humanness with one another, the more we realize that we are not better or worse than anyone.

Awakening is a continuous process. Awakening happens in the now, but there is also always more to awaken. You can arrive now, and you also never arrive fully.

Everyone is perfect, and everyone is a work in progress.

Everyone is an art piece.

To see the perfection in all, see everyone as beauty, love, and truth.

Everyone is already a healer.

Everyone is already a teacher.

Everyone is already loved.

You are the teacher you've been waiting for. Everyone is a teacher they've been waiting for. Together, we teach and learn from one another.

You are the healer you've been waiting for. Everyone is the healer they've been waiting for. Together, we heal ourselves and one another.

You are the love you've been waiting for. Everyone is the love they've been waiting for. Together, we love ourselves and one another.

Love,

Your team

4.6

TRIBUTE TO CARL JUNG

*L*et's close with a few of our favorite quotes paying tribute to the father of Shadow Work in psychology, Carl Jung. He is a total embodiment of Taoist Yin Yang balance!!!

~ Knowing your own darkness is the best method for dealing with the darknesses of other people.

~ Who looks outside, dreams; who looks inside, awakes.

~ Everything that irritates us about others can lead us to an understanding of ourselves.

~ We cannot change anything until we accept it. Condemnation does not liberate, it oppresses.

~ The shoe that fits one person pinches another; there is no recipe for living that suits all cases.

~ The word 'happy' would lose its meaning if it were not balanced by sadness.

~ The healthy man does not torture others - generally, it is the tortured who turn into torturers.

~ Every form of addiction is bad, no matter whether the narcotic is alcohol, morphine, or idealism.

~ The most intense conflicts, if overcome, leave behind a sense of security and calm that is not easily disturbed. It is just these intense conflicts and their conflagration which are needed to produce valuable and lasting results.

~ Children are educated by what the grown-up is and not by his talk.

~ If there is anything that we wish to change in the child, we should first examine it and see whether it is not something that could better be changed in ourselves.

ABOUT THE AUTHOR
WINNIE CHAN WANG

Winnie Chan Wang is a trauma-informed licensed acupuncturist, Reiki practitioner, shadow worker, and shamanic Tao healer. She is also a professor in acupuncture at Alhambra Medical University. In her private practice, Winnie honors her clients as divine self-healers, navigating their healing journeys as co-pilots. Because trauma is the root cause of many physical and emotional illnesses, Winnie focuses on releasing trapped emotions in organs and meridians (energy pathways). Winnie combines the medical science of a clinically trained acupuncturist with the spiritual knowledge of a shaman, to help her clients process their trauma by channeling source healing energy and guided breathwork. Her goal in becoming an author is to guide her readers into a deep self-exploration with compassion and curiosity.

Everyone can heal all aspects of life, including health, relationships, and finances, by aligning their soul, heart, mind, energy, and body. Through sharing stories, she hopes to be a mirror in helping others know themselves and own their authentic source power. Winnie also provides mentoring to other therapists, as spreading healing is her passion and life purpose.

ABOUT THE AUTHOR
JI W. CHOI, M.A.

Ji W. Choi, M.A. is a shadow worker, healer, artist, and doctoral candidate in psychology. Ji earned her Bachelor's degree from Art Center College of Design and has experience in the creative and design field. She received a Master's Degree in clinical psychology from the California School of Professional Psychology at Alliant International University and is currently completing her doctoral degree in psychology (Psy.D.). She is grounded in honoring the interconnectedness of all, while understanding every individual's intersecting layers of identities and unique life experiences. She enjoys leading group healing and meditations to facilitate others' self-discovery collectively collectivistically. She utilizes her strengths of joy, love, and insight to passionately discuss taboo topics in a safe, exploratory way and believes in the sacred medicine of laughter. She is a proud Korean American living in Los Angeles. Honoring Darkness is her first book.

Made in the USA
Columbia, SC
10 April 2022